W9-AAC-835

ERVIN TRASK MEM. LIBRARY
PLAINVILLE HIGH SCHOOL

Family Abuse

A National Epidemic

ERVIN TRASK MEM. LIBRARY
PLAINVILLE HIGH SCHOOL

Maria Hong

—Issues in Focus—

Enslow Publishers, Inc.

44 Fadem Road	PO Box 38
Box 699	Aldershot
Springfield, NJ 07081	Hants GU12 6BP
USA	UK

To the memory of my grandparents, Edwin Blanton Patterson and Frieda Bachschmid Patterson.

Copyright © 1997 by Maria Hong

All rights reserved.

No part of this book may be reproduced by any means without the written permission of the publisher.

Library of Congress Cataloging-in-Publication Data

Hong, Maria.
    Family abuse : a national epidemic / Maria Hong.
        p.   cm. — (Issues in focus)
    Includes bibliographical references and index.
    Summary: Discusses many forms of family abuse, including child abuse, sexual abuse, and domestic violence.
    ISBN 0-89490-720-4
    1. Family violence—United States—Juvenile literature. 2. Child abuse—United States—Juvenile literature. [1. Child abuse. 2. Family violence.]
    I. Title. II. Series: Issues in focus (Hillside, N.J.)
    HV6626.2.H66 1997
    362.82'92—dc21
                                    97-7906
                                      CIP
                                      AC

Printed in the United States of America

10 9 8 7 6 5 4 3 2 1

The quotation from Jane Marks's article "We Have a Problem," *Parents*, is reprinted by permission of Jane Marks, the author of *The Hidden Children: The Secret Survivors of the Holocaust* (Balantine). The quotation from D. G. from "What's Love Got to Do With It?" is reprinted by permission of *Ms.* magazine, © 1994. The quotation from Rosemary L. Bray from "Remember the Children" is reprinted by permission of *Ms.* magazine, © 1994. The quotation from Robert L. Allen and Paul Kivel from "Men Changing Men" is reprinted by permission of *Ms.* magazine, © 1994.

Cover Illustration: Josie Seeligson

Contents

Acknowledgments

I would like to thank Wendy Varnell, Char Bateman, Judith Cornelius, and Diane Crosson for taking the time to speak with me about their work and enriching this book with their expertise. I am deeply grateful to Seriya Stone for bravely and eloquently lending his story to the book. I would also like to thank Deborah Tharinger for pointing me to people working on family abuse issues in Travis County. And without the unflagging support of generous and sometimes sleep-deprived friends and family in New York and Austin this project never would have been realized. To all of you who gave me hope, humor, and wisdom, my most heartfelt thanks and love.

At best, the family teaches the finest things human beings can learn from one another—generosity and love. But it is also, all too often, where we learn nasty things like hate and rage and shame.[1]

—Barbara Ehrenreich, author of *The Snarling Citizen*

1

Family Abuse: A National Epidemic

On the morning of Thanksgiving Day, 1995, police officers, firefighters, and paramedics in New York City responded to an emergency call that a little girl had stopped breathing. When they arrived at the Rutgers House housing project on Manhattan's Lower East Side, they found six-year-old Elisa Izquierdo in her bed, dead from a brain hemorrhage caused by trauma to her head. Her body showed signs of years of abuse.

When the police arrived at the scene, Elisa's mother, Awilda Lopez, confessed to killing Elisa by slamming her against a concrete wall the day before. Ms. Lopez said that she believed Elisa was possessed by the devil. Round marks covering Elisa's body turned out to be welts left by the stone in a ring worn by someone who had hit her. Law enforcement authorities later found that she also had been repeatedly sexually assaulted. Police Lieutenant Luis

Gonzalez stated, "In my 22 years, this is the worst case of child abuse I have ever seen."[2] Awilda Lopez was charged with murder, manslaughter, and endangering the welfare of Elisa and two of her other children. Carlos Lopez, Elisa's stepfather, was charged with assault in beating Elisa. Both parents were accused of a pattern of abusing Elisa from May 1, 1994, through November 23, 1995, the day she died.

Elisa Izquierdo's tragic case riveted the nation not only because of the extreme nature of the horrors she suffered but also because her murder and abuse could have been prevented. Before her death, Elisa's case had come to the attention of New York City's Administration for Children's Services at least eight times. The ACS, which is responsible for investigating child abuse cases in the city, first heard about Elisa when she was born on February 11, 1989. Awilda Lopez was a crack cocaine addict and when Elisa was born addicted to drugs, hospital social workers alerted the ACS as part of standard procedure. They gave custody rights to Elisa's father, Gustavo Izquierdo.

Gustavo Izquierdo was by all accounts a devoted and doting parent. Elisa lived with him until he died of cancer in 1994. After his death, Judge Phoebe K. Greenbaum awarded temporary custody to Awilda Lopez, despite previous reports to social services that she had abused Elisa during weekend visits. Social service authorities also knew that Carlos Lopez had gone to prison for stabbing Awilda seventeen times with a pocket knife in 1992. Elsa Canizares, one of Gustavo Izquierdo's cousins, had tried to get custody of Elisa, but the court ruled in favor of the

Lopezes. Laws and social service agencies generally try to keep biological families together.

From 1990 to 1995, neighbors, teachers, school officials, and relatives reported their observations of Elisa's abuse to state and city child welfare agencies. ACS caseworkers visited the Lopez home but did not find sufficient evidence to remove her. One person who had called Elisa's caseworker about suspicions of abuse said that the caseworker never responded to repeated calls and said he was "too busy" to go by the home.[3]

Like the murder of Lisa Steinberg by her father Joel Steinberg in 1987, Elisa's case had one positive effect: focusing public attention on the problem of child abuse. As details of her situation emerged, many people expressed outrage and wondered how such a tragedy could have been allowed to occur. Newspaper and magazine articles noted how massive cuts in funding to social services have produced a child welfare system that is greatly overburdened, with caseworkers handling too many cases at a time and receiving pressure to close cases prematurely. The attention generated by Elisa's terrible story spurred some changes in legislation and in the city's child welfare system.[4]

Widespread Family Violence

Unfortunately, Elisa Izquierdo's case, though extreme, is far from unique. Millions of children suffer torture at the hands of their parents and other family members each year. And, as in Elisa's situation, other forms of family violence, such as partner abuse, frequently occur at the same time. Family abuse in all its forms is a phenomenon that has gained increasing attention as a widespread problem.

In 1991, former U.S. Surgeon General Antonia C. Novello called family violence "an epidemic in America."[5] Although it is impossible to determine accurate statistics on family abuse due to underreporting, even conservative estimates are startling. According to a 1984 U. S. Department of Justice report, at least 4.1 million cases of family violence occurred between 1973 and 1981, an average of 450,000 per year. And FBI statistics estimate that nearly 20 percent of all murders are committed by family members.[6]

Every year, child protective service agencies receive more than 2.5 million reports of alleged child abuse or neglect. One third to one half of all women are estimated to be physically abused by a male partner at some point during their lives. About 5 percent of people over age sixty-five are thought to suffer elder abuse, with two thirds of the abusers being family members.[7]

Family abuse has a devastating impact on both the people who experience it and society. People who are mistreated by family members suffer from physical injuries ranging from bruises to lifelong impairment. Abuse can also result in depression, anxiety, and other psychological problems. Sometimes victims' feelings of hopelessness and despair give rise to destructive actions such as abusing drugs, attempting suicide, and becoming violent toward others. Violent youths are four times more likely than nonviolent teenagers to come from homes where mothers were beaten by fathers. And although women commit only 8 percent of homicides in the United States, over half of those murders are against an abusive partner.[8]

Family abuse also creates an enormous drain on

public institutions such as hospitals and law enforcement. The medical costs of reported family-violence-related injuries are estimated to be about $44.4 million a year. Thirty-five percent of women visiting hospital emergency rooms are there for symptoms due to partner abuse. Twenty-five to fifty percent of homeless families are headed by women who left home to escape domestic violence. It is estimated that we spend $5 to $10 billion a year on the social costs of family violence.[9]

In this book, we will examine family abuse as a widespread problem that affects individuals and their communities. Most of the chapters will focus on different forms of abuse, such as child abuse and neglect, domestic violence, and elder abuse. But before getting into specifics, it may be helpful to discuss some of the terms, patterns, and misconceptions that relate to all forms of family abuse.

What Is Family Abuse?

The term *family abuse* refers to acts of violence and abuse committed by one family member against another. Although experts have used the terms *violence* and *abuse* in different ways, most people use these terms to refer to distinct types of behavior.

Violence can be defined as aggressive behavior that results or could result in injury, harm, or destruction. Most often it refers to physically damaging acts such as hitting, slapping, beating, burning, and using a weapon. When used against family members, violence can harm the victim's potential to grow and develop.

Abuse is a broader term, which refers to both physical

violence and other forms of mistreatment that can result in nonphysical harm. Abusive behavior can be psychological and nonviolent, such as insulting or embarrassing someone. Abuse also refers to acts of sexual abuse and neglect. Sexually abusive acts include fondling, inappropriate exposure, and marital rape (forced sex in marriage). Neglect is defined as failure to provide someone you are responsible for with necessary care and protection, as when a parent leaves a young child unsupervised for long periods of time.

Family abuse occurs when a person commits abusive or violent acts against a family member. *Family members* include any biological, step-, or foster family member: fathers, mothers, children, uncles, aunts, cousins, brothers, sisters, grandparents, and in-laws. Sometimes the term *family violence* is used interchangeably with family abuse. The term *domestic violence* is also sometimes used to mean any violence occurring in the home. However, in this book, domestic violence will refer specifically to partner abuse. The words *maltreatment* and *mistreatment* are also frequently used to refer to acts that are either violent or abusive.

Family abuse is nothing new. What has changed in the last few decades is public awareness and attitudes toward family members mistreating each other. In order to understand how public responses to abuse affect victims and perpetrators, it is important to know something about the history of family abuse.

A Brief History of Family Violence

Child abuse and domestic violence have long, documented histories as accepted practices in many cultures. Infanticide, which is the most widely studied form of family violence, was traditionally accepted as a way of getting rid of unwanted babies in Europe during the Middle Ages and in many ancient civilizations. The Hebrew code of 800 B.C. and the Hammurabi code of 2100 B.C. considered infanticide acceptable.[10] For centuries, the practice of using beatings to discipline children was supported by the Bible's famous proverb, "Spare the rod and spoil the child."

There is also evidence of violence against adult female family members in ancient societies. In 1985, medical paleopathologists found a higher incidence of fractures among women than in men—50 percent compared with 20 percent—in mummies two to three thousand years old. They determined that the fractures were caused by lethal blows resulting from peacetime personal violence. Theodora, Justinian's empress of Byzantium from A.D. 508–548, was one of the first people in recorded history to speak out against spousal abuse.[11]

It was not until the early part of the twentieth century that it became illegal in the United States for women and children to be beaten by their husbands or parents. With its basis in English Common Law, the U.S. legal system had historically viewed women and children as the property of the male head of the household. He could use physical abuse as a means to control other family members. A modified version of the "Rule of Thumb" law, which allowed a husband to beat his wife with a stick no wider than the circumference of his thumb, was upheld in a Mississippi court as recently as 1928.[12]

However, attitudes toward family abuse began to change in the United States during the mid-nineteenth century. In 1882, Maryland became the first state to make wife-beating a punishable crime. And in 1871, the beating of a nine-year-old girl named Mary Ellen by her adoptive parents in New York City helped make child abuse a public concern. Neighbors brought her case to the attention of the Society for the Prevention of Cruelty to Animals, which was the only organization that could remedy the situation at the time. The Society succeeded in removing the girl from her parents' custody by saying that she was a member of the animal kingdom and her parents had violated existing laws against animal cruelty. Soon after this case was investigated, the Society for the Prevention of Cruelty to Children was founded.

In 1906, pediatric radiology began and the technology of X rays made it possible to detect and document physical injuries resulting from abuse. In 1925, the New York Society for the Reformation of Juvenile Delinquents established a home that served runaway, neglected, and abused children. Dr. C. Henry Kempe focused national attention on the problem of child abuse in 1961 when he described the "battered child syndrome" at a meeting of the American Academy of Pediatrics.[13]

Recognizing the Problems

Ever since Dr. Kempe's presentation of his findings on the effects of child abuse, there has been growing recognition of child maltreatment as a significant problem. Since 1968, all states have required reporting of child abuse.[14] In 1974, the federal government enacted the Child Abuse Prevention and Treatment Act and established the National Center on Child Abuse and

Neglect to help stop child maltreatment. During the late 1960s and 1970s, the women's movement helped to focus attention on child sexual abuse, rape, and domestic violence.

Society was slower to recognize partner abuse as a social problem than it was to recognize child abuse. Many people felt women consented to the abuse and believed that husbands had the right to control their wives through violence. However, during the 1970s, the feminist political movement gave rise to the concerns of domestic violence victims, establishing what became known as the battered women's movement. At first, people working to help battered women opened up their own homes to help victims escape from violence. Later, the need for domestic violence shelters became apparent and shelters were founded throughout the country. Other services such as emergency hotlines, information and referral, counseling for battered women and batterers, community education, and advocacy within social service and legal systems have grown tremendously over the last twenty-five years.

Elder abuse first emerged as a public concern in 1979, when a group of Boston researchers found that elder abuse was a problem among a significant portion of the population. During the early 1980s, congressional hearings further emphasized the need to address elder abuse as a widespread problem.

As you read this book, it may be helpful to remember how the responses of institutions and people outside the family can help victims of family abuse. In the final chapter, we will look at some recent responses to family violence.

Forms of Family Abuse

The main forms of family abuse—physical abuse, sexual abuse, emotional abuse, and neglect—will be discussed more fully in chapters 2 to 4, since such behaviors vary depending on the relationship between the abuser and the victim. In those chapters, we will examine child abuse and neglect, domestic violence, elder abuse, parent abuse, and sibling abuse. For each type of abuse, we will look at definitions, the impact on victims, risk factors, and common patterns of abuse. Child maltreatment and domestic violence are discussed more than the other types because they affect children and teenagers more directly and more frequently. Chapters 2 and 3 include sections on teenage victims of abuse.

Although family abuse occurs in many different forms, the impact of abuse on victims and the reactions of outsiders can be strikingly similar from situation to situation. Violence is known to result in further violence, and very often, there is more than one type of abuse occurring within a family.[15] By examining different types of family abuse together, we may achieve a better understanding of the causes, consequences, and dynamics of abuse as it occurs in daily life.

As you read about each type of abuse, it is important to remember that anyone can be a victim of family violence. People of all ages, races, ethnic groups, regions, religions, and socioeconomic levels suffer maltreatment from family members. The last chapter of this book focuses on how different aspects of society have responded to family abuse, highlighting prevention and intervention efforts and what you can do to help solve the problem.

Myths Distort Facts About Abuse

Certain myths have traditionally made it hard to prevent family abuse from happening. These misconceptions include the following:

- Family abuse is very rare.
- It occurs only within poor families and certain racial and ethnic groups.
- It is perpetrated only by mentally ill or alcohol- or drug-abusing persons.
- Victims of abuse provoke it and should be blamed for it.

Since much of the discussion will be devoted to the consequences of mistreatment, it may be good to keep in mind that while family abuse is a widespread problem, many families maintain healthy relationships. In healthy or functional families, parents and other caregivers respond to the needs of more vulnerable members like children, maintain effective communication, respect individual choice and privacy, and foster the growth of each person's interests and abilities. By understanding family abuse better, we may be able to encourage the development of the family as a place of true support for everyone.

It's an outrage that we receive more than 2.5 million reports of child abuse and neglect every year. . . . This is not only sad; it's a national crime and our collective shame.[1]

—Donna E. Shalala, secretary of the
Department of Health and Human Services

2

Child Abuse and Neglect

For Seriya Stone,* a graduate student and writer, family get-togethers could become unpleasant occasions:

> We would all come together at family gatherings. All of us cousins would do things and get whipped by our fathers. But when my father would whip me, he would take me back to a room and everyone would be in the front room and there would be silence and everyone would just be listening to my father beat me. Until this day you could ask family members and they'll tell you how the way my father used to beat me just kind of set everyone's teeth on edge. It was different from what my cousins experienced, and I mean, I'm different—I'm more disciplined, I'm more controlled, I'm more successful, but I don't know what the price has been. I'm having to process all this now.[2]

Now in his twenties, Seriya Stone recalled how his father, an airplane technician and technical trainer for the

---

*The name has been changed to protect his identity.

17

U.S. Air Force, regularly beat him while he was growing up, sometimes kicking him or using a belt. Although Stone suffered frequent, sometimes weekly, "whippings" from him, he said that the main target of his father's violence was his mother. He described his father as an alcoholic who, after going out drinking, would often hit and beat his mother.

> He would come in drunk, cussing at my mom, fighting with my mom. . . . Sometimes it was once a week, sometimes it was three times a week. It started when I was around two or three years old. Sometimes if he was doing fine, it was maybe once a month.[3]

Stone's mother also whipped him as a form of discipline, sometimes making him take his pants down and lean over a bathtub, although his father beat him with more force and malice. As a result of the violence in his family, Stone said that he himself became violent, frequently fighting with other children at school and hitting his younger brother, who was not beaten as severely by their father.

More than the physical pain, Stone emphasized that he felt the emotional impact of his father's abusiveness and his absence as a parent.

> There was always a subtle fear I had of my father, like if I said something wrong or if I did something just wrong, and he was not in the right mood, then I would be in trouble. . . . When I was ten or eleven I would cry all the time. I would cry myself into headaches, because I would get so angry at my father that I couldn't get it out any other way.[4]

The whippings became less frequent as Stone got older, and the violence ended when his mother left his father while Stone was a teenager. However, the physical and emotional abuse Stone experienced and witnessed had long-lasting repercussions:

> I think a big part of it is that your personality just splits and there are parts of yourself that you're just not conscious of. And the part that's not acknowledged will come out in rage and for me sometimes it results in depression. . . . That's the long term effect of it.

Stone, who is African-American, added that he believes that sometimes family violence can be traced back to the institutionalized violence of slavery. "I think a lot of African Americans of all classes deal with this internalization of violence, with a large portion of it being historical."[5]

The Secret Crime

Like many other survivors of abuse, Stone has grappled with being intimidated into not speaking about what happened to him. Due to feelings of fear and shame and lack of knowledge about where to go for help, most abused children do not talk about what has happened to them. As a result, child abuse and neglect cases remain tremendously underreported. However, estimates based on the number of reports to the police, child protective agencies, and other authorities reflect the magnitude of the problem.

Every year, more than 2.5 million children are reported to child welfare agencies in the United States as alleged victims of child abuse or neglect.[6] In 1993, 2,989,000 children were reported to child protective agencies for maltreatment, and about 1,016,000 cases of child abuse and neglect were confirmed by these agencies. At least three children a day die from child abuse and neglect in the United States, and an estimated 1,299 children were reported as dying from abuse or neglect in 1993.[7] Since many incidents are never reported or are misrepresented as accidents, these figures represent only a small portion of actual cases.

Although some child abuse incidents are committed by strangers, about 85 percent of them are perpetrated by someone the child knows, usually his or her parent.[8] According to some sources, about 2 to 4 million children suffer abuse or neglect from a parent each year. An estimated two hundred thousand to five hundred thousand children are sexually abused by family members annually. And about two thousand to five thousand children are killed each year by their parents.[9]

These grim statistics underscore the extent of child abuse and neglect as nationwide problems. In this chapter, we will discuss different forms of child mistreatment, the impact of abuse on victims, and some of the factors associated with child abuse and neglect. Since many victims of abuse are teenagers, there will also be a section on adolescent abuse.

What Is Child Abuse?

The National Council on Child Abuse and Family Violence defines child abuse as any behavior directed toward a child by an adult that endangers or impairs his or her physical or emotional health and development. A child is a person under the age of eighteen. An abused or neglected child is one whose welfare is harmed or threatened by acts or omissions by his or her parents or other caregivers. There are four main categories of child maltreatment: physical abuse, sexual abuse, emotional abuse, and neglect.

Physical Abuse. When many people think of child abuse, they imagine a child like Elisa Izquierdo who has been tortured and severely beaten by her parents. This type of maltreatment falls under the category of physical abuse. Physical abuse involves acts that cause or could have caused physical injury or pain to the child. Physical abuse does not necessarily involve the intention to hurt the child, since injury can occur during punishment that is inappropriate to the child's age or is excessive, as in Seriya Stone's case.

Different cultural definitions of acceptable behaviors have created debate over which acts should be considered physically abusive. For example, according to some definitions, spanking is considered physically abusive, because it generally causes pain and the intent of the action is to cause the child some harm in order to send a message. However, other definitions do not include spanking as a form of physical abuse, because it is considered socially acceptable and even appropriate by many people. Perhaps the best way to determine whether or not acts are physically abusive is to apply the same standards that are used to judge acts committed by strangers to those perpetrated by family members.

Even when only very harsh acts are considered, the incidence of physical abuse remains high. According to a 1995 nationwide poll of parents, more than 3 million children are physically abused in the name of discipline each year. The acts that were classified as abusive in the study were punching, kicking, throwing the child down, or hitting with a hard object on a part of the body other than the bottom.[10] Actions such as spanking and slapping were not classified as physically abusive in the survey. Other physically abusive acts include beating, burning, immersion in scalding water, biting, and assaults with objects or weapons such as knives or guns.

Although physical abuse is the form of child mistreatment that is most easily recognized by people outside the family, other forms of abuse are just as harmful to the health and development of children. One form of abuse that has received growing public attention since the 1970s is child sexual abuse.

Sexual Abuse. Alan Trager, the assistant executive director of Westchester Jewish Community Services and founder of the Child Sexual Abuse Treatment Center, has worked with many young people who have experienced sexual abuse. Here is the story of one of his patients:

> It was last year at Grandpa's house in Pennsylvania—right after Grandma's funeral," Pam said. She had found her grandfather crying in his bedroom. "Oh, Pam," he sobbed, "I'm so alone." He hugged her very hard—and then he took her hand and placed it on his penis.
>
> Soon he wanted her to fondle him whenever he could get her alone. One time he put his hand up Pam's skirt, but she cried, so he stopped and didn't try it again. But he still wanted her to touch him.
>
> Pam said she *knew* it was wrong. She hated touching Clay, and she hated and resented him for making her do it. But she also felt that he was very important to the family. And she believed him when he told her that her "loving" him was all he had to live for.[11]

Pam's situation came to the attention of her parents when her mother Lucy Ingram came home early from work one day and found her father-in-law Clay molesting Pam. Lucy and her husband Joel, who ran a business together in the affluent suburb of Westchester, New York, were shocked, confused, and outraged by the discovery. Luckily, they soon contacted Alan Trager, a therapist who specializes in helping children who have been sexually abused, and they got help for Pam and themselves. Pam seemed to feel relieved when the secret was finally out, and she was able to recover from the abuse with her parents' support. Lucy and Joel also confronted Clay, who at first denied the abuse, but then later admitted to it and agreed to get therapeutic help himself. After several months without contact, the Ingrams met with Clay, who apologized to Pam and her parents. He also told Lucy and Joel that he had abused other young girls and that he never would have gotten professional help for his problem if they had not insisted that he do so.[12]

Cases of sexual abuse such as this represent a commonly hidden yet widespread form of child maltreatment. Three fourths of the crimes committed against children are sex crimes.[13] Yet because of the secrecy and shame associated with child sexual abuse, this type of abuse may be even more underreported than other forms. About 150,000 substantiated cases of sexual abuse, representing 15 percent of child abuse cases, were reported to child welfare authorities in 1993. Researchers estimate that about one in four girls and one out of every seven or eight boys will be sexually abused before the age of eighteen. According to surveys of adult survivors of child sexual abuse, which may be more accurate than

23

studies based on child reports, there are about five hundred thousand new cases of child sexual abuse each year.[14]

Sexual abuse can be defined as the exploitation of a child for the sexual gratification or financial benefit of an adult caregiver. A caregiver is someone who is responsible for the child's well-being, like a teacher, baby-sitter, or family member. However, when the abuser is not a family member, the violation is considered *sexual assault* rather than sexual abuse and these cases are handled differently under the law of many states.

Most sexual abuse is committed by someone the child knows. About one third to one half of the people who sexually abuse girls and 10 percent to 20 percent of those who abuse boys are family members.[15] When the abuser is someone within the victim's family, such as the child's parent, stepparent, sibling, cousin, uncle, aunt, grandparent, or in-law, the sexual abuse can also be called incest. In cases of sexual abuse and assault, the adult is always completely responsible for the sexual activity. Sometimes the abuser believes the child is willing to participate, but it is impossible for a child to consent to sexual acts because of the differences in age, knowledge, and power between the adult and child. A child who agrees to an older person's demands may be doing so out of a sense of duty, obligation, obedience, or fear, or because she or he lacks knowledge about what is going on.

Sexual abuse and incest include sexual contact such as touching the sexual parts of the victim's body like the genitals or breasts; demanding that the child touch the abuser's body; penetration of the victim's vagina, mouth, or anus with the penis, hands, or objects; sexual kissing;

and use of the child in prostitution. Abuse also includes exposing the child to sexual issues that are not appropriate for his or her age and raising the child in a sexually provocative environment. Some examples of noncontact abusive behaviors are exhibitionism, which occurs when the abuser exposes his or her body to the child; voyeurism or demanding to see the child naked or partially undressed; making lewd comments about the child's body; masturbating or having sex in front of the child; showing pornography; and taking photographs of the child for use in pornography.

Sometimes exposure is abusive and sometimes it is not. In some families, nudity among family members within the home is acceptable, and sometimes it is unavoidable if family members share a small space with limited privacy. Exposure is considered abusive when the adult is sexually aroused by the act and does it for that purpose.

In some cases, such as rape or grabbing a child's body, the abuser uses violence or physical force to sexually attack the victim. In these cases, the child or adolescent may feel powerless to fight off the abuser and may fear that he or she will not physically survive the assault. However, in many situations, sexual abuse does not involve the use of physical force. Children can be misled, bribed, or verbally forced into complying with the abuser's demands. Because children are taught to respect and obey adults, are naturally curious, and need affection and attention, they may misunderstand abuse as a way to receive that support. The perpetrator may also attempt to spare the child physical pain while using the child to fulfill his or her sexual needs, without acknowledging the trauma he or she is causing the victim. In some instances

25

the abuse is disguised as care, as when a parent gives a child intrusive and unnecessary enemas or genital exams or washes a child's genitals excessively while bathing the child. Even when the parents or other family members are not consciously using the child for sexual purposes, the acts may be abusive if they violate community standards or impair the child's sexual development.

Acts of sexual abuse and incest may occur once or be repeated over many years. In all cases, child sexual abuse and incest can have devastating effects on victims. And both physical and sexual maltreatment are also closely linked with emotional abuse and neglect.

Emotional Abuse. Emotional abuse or psychological abuse consists of words and actions that undermine or would generally be expected to undermine a child's sense of self-worth, competence, and security. It often occurs when parents or other caregivers make excessive or unreasonable demands on their children, based on expectations that are beyond the child's capabilities.

Often, emotional maltreatment is expressed as *verbal abuse*: words said to the child or made in the presence of the child that are either intended to be wounding or would reasonably be viewed as harmful. Verbal abuse includes name calling, making belittling or demeaning remarks, constant teasing, threatening with physical harm, blaming the child for the adult's problems, being unfairly critical or sarcastic, and insulting and verbally intimidating the child.

Emotional abuse can also involve withholding positive emotional support necessary for a child's development. In addition to material things, children need love, affection, care, and guidance in order to grow

26

in healthy ways. When parents fail to provide psychological nurturance, children may experience emotionally painful and harmful consequences.

Emotionally abusive messages are frequently complex and hard to recognize. Such remarks, actions, or lack of action tell children that they are not valued for themselves, that they cannot meet their parents expectations no matter what they do, and that their needs are unimportant.

Verbal abuse usually accompanies physical or sexual abuse. Physically and sexually abusive acts are also emotionally abusive in themselves. They destroy the victim's sense of trust and security in his or her family and can damage the child's development and ability to form other relationships. A parent who refuses to believe a child who says that he or she is being sexually abused by another family member commits emotional abuse by not supporting the child when he or she needs it.

Some researchers use the term *emotional incest* to refer to situations in which a parent emotionally treats a child like a spouse. In these cases, the parent looks to his or her child for guidance or as a confidant, discussing adult problems such as issues related to sexuality or relationships. The child is expected to nurture the parent and protect him or her, sometimes against the aggression of the other parent. This subtle form of abuse places a burden on the child, creating stress and confusion, since children are not prepared to act as adults or to take care of their parents.

Emotional abuse is the most difficult form of abuse for outsiders to recognize and verify, since it does not leave visible physical scars. For the same reasons, it is also often difficult for victims of emotional maltreatment to identify it as abuse. However, by itself or in combination with other forms of abuse it can have extremely negative effects that persist for years. It is also closely related to the fourth major form of maltreatment: neglect.

Neglect. Neglect is the most common form of child maltreatment to be reported and substantiated by child protective agencies, and it represents 47 percent of confirmed cases.[16] Neglect is defined as the continued withholding of or failure to provide necessary care and protection. Parents and primary caregivers who act as parents are required by law to provide food, clothing, medical care, and a safe home environment for their children. When parents fail to provide these things they commit neglect.

Neglect occurs when a parent does not take care of his or her child's hygiene and health; leaves a child, especially a young child, without appropriate supervision; or fails to give a child the care needed for ideal growth and development, despite the financial ability to do so. If the parent is financially incapable of providing necessary care, failing to find other ways of providing for the child is considered neglect.

Emotional neglect can be considered a form of emotional abuse (and vice versa) since children need emotional as well as physical care. Children need encouragement to feel like valuable people who can trust others, perform in school, develop skills, and enjoy life. Support may be communicated through words or appropriate affectionate actions such as being held, cuddled, kissed, having their hands shaken, and being patted on the back. Parents need to take the time to listen to their children and comfort and help them when necessary. Emotional neglect occurs when parents fail to give their children this kind of support. Often, neglect is unintentional. For example, in cases where a parent physically abuses his or her spouse and the children, the abused parent is still responsible for providing a safe environment for the children but may not be able to do so.

In most cases, several forms of abuse operate at the same time in a family and usually there is more than one instance of maltreatment. The milder forms of maltreatment are more common, but every form can have long-lasting, harmful effects on victims.

The Impact of Child Abuse and Neglect

Oprah Winfrey, talk-show host, actor, and producer, has shared her experiences of being abused as a child with the public: "I know what it's like to be a silent victim of child abuse. I blamed myself for most of my adult life. You lose your childhood once you've been abused. Your life changes forever."[17]

Victims of physical child abuse may suffer from bruises, welts, burns, abrasions, cuts, fractures, and broken bones. Sometimes doctors can identify such injuries as the result of abuse rather than accidents by their location on the body. Unexplained injuries caused by abuse often appear on the eyes, mouth, back, thighs, buttocks, and genital areas, rather than the arms and legs where injuries from normal childhood activities generally occur. Other signs of abuse are injuries or scars that show the shape of objects used to hurt the child, like belts or cigarette burns. A study conducted by the Centers for

Disease Control concluded that abuse was a major leading cause of developmental disabilities among children, second only to bacterial meningitis.[18]

Sexual abuse can also have harmful physical effects such as cuts, bruises, genital swelling, chronic urinary tract infections, venereal disease, and pregnancy. The teen pregnancy rate is especially high among sexually abused teenagers. In one study, 66 percent of pregnant adolescents reported being sexually abused at some point, and 11 percent reported becoming pregnant as a result of assault, usually incestuous.[19]

Physical abuse, sexual abuse, emotional abuse, and neglect can also be very psychologically traumatic to victims. However, there is no typical emotional reaction or type of behavior that indicates abuse. A child's reactions to abuse depend on his or her personal characteristics, relationships with other family members and outsiders, and the specific circumstances of abuse.

Reactions to Abuse

Some abused children draw inward, becoming socially isolated. Others act out aggressively by lying, stealing, yelling frequently, or fighting. Other common consequences of abuse include lowered self-confidence and self-esteem; a sense of worthlessness and inadequacy; learning difficulties; distrust of adults; troubled relationships with peers; lack of empathy for others; feelings of betrayal, guilt, and shame; and depression. Like other people who have suffered severe trauma, abused children may also experience symptoms similar to post-traumatic stress disorder (PTSD). (See box on PTSD, page 34.)

Some victims of child abuse try to avoid thoughts, feelings, and situations that might remind them of past abuse. They may experience a sense of detachment or dissociation from their feelings and bodies. Some abuse survivors develop a kind of amnesia, in which they cannot remember aspects of the trauma they have experienced. This often happens if the abuse occurs when the victim is very young or if he or she has suffered sexual abuse. In these situations, memories of childhood abuse don't surface until later when the survivor is better equipped to deal with the abuse.

Child sexual abuse within families frequently lasts over a long period of time. Children and adolescents who are sexually abused by family members may feel ashamed because they have a sense that what is going on is wrong or condemned by society, even if they do not fully understand the abuser's behavior. Some survivors report a sense of isolation, difficulties trusting others, fears about parenting, and disturbances in adult sexual relations that persist when they are grown up. Children who have been sexually abused may act seductively toward adults and other children or may act out sexually.

Often, the perpetrator will tell the child that the abuse is a secret that they shouldn't talk about, sometimes threatening to hurt the child or his or her loved ones or pets if he or she does talk about it. Even when no threats are made, victims usually do not tell anyone because they blame themselves and believe that others will think they are bad. When the abuser is a close relative, the child may not tell anyone because she or he feels that the abuser is an important family member and does not want the abuser or the family to be hurt. The victim may also start to doubt his or her perception of what is happening or what happened, since he or she is forced to choose between trusting himself or herself and believing an adult whom he or she is supposed to trust.

Society also pays a price for maltreatment. Child sexual abuse is cited as one of the three main reasons that children run away from home; 70 percent of teenage drug addicts have experienced sexual abuse within their families; and 66 percent to 75 percent of adolescent prostitutes are victims of incest.[20]

It is important to remember that all forms of maltreatment have serious consequences. Some researchers have found that neglect can be more disturbing than physical abuse in certain cases, especially among very young children and infants.

There has been debate over the "cycle of violence" theory—the idea that abuse is transmitted from one generation to another. Although some studies show that child abuse increases the risk of becoming an abusive or violent adult, most abused and neglected children do not become delinquent, criminal, or abusive people. As Wendy D. Varnell, a social worker who coordinates a program that helps abused and neglected teenagers, noted:

> Some teens take that energy and channel it, so they excel in school; some of them are fantastic athletes. They really drive themselves, which is great for them now although it may cause problems when they're adults. I see some incredibly motivated kids. There's no single reaction or consequence. Some kids who have been abused and come through it, develop a lot of compassion for other people, so that's a really positive consequence.[21]

Since every child is different and there are frequently no physical signs of maltreatment, professionals working to prevent child abuse often cannot identify victims easily. In the next section, we will look at who is most at risk for being mistreated.

Victims of Child Maltreatment

Judith Cornelius, a clinical director at the Travis County Children's Advocacy Center, warns that:

> Any kid's at risk, because children are raised in this culture to respect and acquiesce to the authority of adults. How many times has Uncle Johnny come over and Mom or Dad has insisted that you go over and give him a hug or give him a kiss and the kid's not comfortable with it? Well, that's sort of an inkling of what the general context is for kids, the expectation of the way to interact with adults. There's an incredible imbalance of power, and of course there should be to a certain degree, but kids should not be forced to have any sort of physical contact or be left alone with someone that they're not comfortable with.[22]

Anyone can become a victim of child abuse or neglect. Children of all ages, races, ethnic groups, geographic locations, religions, and socioeconomic levels suffer maltreatment from their parents and other family members. Although professionals working on abuse issues try to focus on prevention, determining who is most at risk for abuse has been difficult. For example, early research suggested that certain child and infant characteristics such as low birth weight, premature birth, poor health status, and having disabilities enhanced the

Post-Traumatic Stress Disorder

Battered women, abused children, and children who witness domestic violence have been known to suffer from a range of psychological symptoms identified as post-traumatic stress disorder (PTSD). First linked with the horrifying experiences of soldiers who fought in the Vietnam War, PTSD affects people who have experienced prolonged violence and who have developed certain psychological responses to ongoing trauma. During assaults, victims of violence may focus on self-protection or survival and experience shock, withdrawal, numbing, denial, confusion, and fear. People with PTSD often feel like they are reexperiencing traumatic events, even when they are not occurring. In between violent attacks, they may suffer nightmares about violence; difficulties falling asleep, staying asleep, or concentrating; hallucinations; flashbacks to previous instances of abuse; anxiety attacks; psychosomatic disorders like constant headaches or ulcers; hypervigilance; lack of energy and passivity; feelings of constant terror and impending disaster; a sense of helplessness and despair; and the belief that they deserve the abuse. Victims may also come to believe that their futures will be bleak, without hope of enjoyable work or relationships. Besides family violence victims, other people who have been documented to experience PTSD include prisoners of war and hostages.

risk of abuse, but recent studies have contradicted these findings.

Similarly, research reveals conflicting conclusions about the numbers of male and female victims of physical abuse, emotional abuse, and neglect. Some studies state that more boys are abused, while other studies show no differences in rates of abuse based on gender.

However, in one area, child sexual abuse, girls are more often reported as victims than boys at all ages. Some studies estimate that there are three times as many sexually abused girls as boys.[23] Male sexual abuse victims also seem to be abused more often outside of the home, whereas girls are more often victimized by family members.

The gap between the numbers of boys and girls reported as sexually abused can be partly explained by male victims' greater reluctance to tell people about the abuse. Boys may feel more ashamed about being abused, since stereotypes about being male put pressure on them to act strong and invincible at all times. Also, most sexual abuse of both boys and girls is committed by men. Boys who are abused by men may fear that they will be seen as homosexual if they reveal the abuse and boys who are victimized by women may think that the abuse is somehow acceptable. Adults may be less inclined to believe a boy who says he has been sexually abused than a girl.

Some studies show that about one quarter of all child sexual abuse occurs before the age of seven. However, the average age at which boys and girls are first sexually abused is around ten, and most sexual abuse victims are older than other child abuse and neglect victims.[24]

Teenagers represent a significant number of the youths who suffer sexual abuse and other forms of family abuse.

Adolescent Abuse

According to Wendy D. Varnell, a coordinator at a child mental health center, claims of abuse from teenagers are often not taken as seriously as those from children.

> I think it's a very tricky situation when a teen is disclosing abuse, because with younger, more vulnerable children there's quicker response. The younger child will be removed from the situation or the situation will be intervened. With a teenager there's the perception that the teen has done something to cause the abuse, because teenagers are very intimidating in general. People sometimes see a runaway and think that person has just chosen to run away, but often that teenager has left home because the situation was unbearable.[25]

Abuse of adolescents is one of the most overlooked areas of family abuse. Usually, when people think of child maltreatment, they imagine a small, young child being abused by a much larger, stronger adult. However, research has shown that adolescents suffer a high proportion of abuse, including severe forms of physical abuse that cause injuries and death. In 1990, more than 208,000 adolescents were reported to child protective service agencies as victims of abuse. They represented 25 percent of reported child maltreatment cases. The number of reported cases of adolescent abuse has increased steadily since 1976.[26]

Teenagers generally experience abuse and neglect at the same rate as or at higher rates than younger children.

According to a study by the National Center on Child Abuse and Neglect, adolescents between the ages of twelve and seventeen make up about 38 percent of the child population, yet they constitute 47 percent of the child abuse victims. Older youth between the ages of fifteen and seventeen make up 19 percent of the child population but are the victims of 27 percent of the serious injuries and 23 percent of the fatalities due to maltreatment.[27]

Although they experience higher rates of abuse than younger victims, teenagers who suffer abuse are less likely to be identified as abused since they usually suffer less physical damage and are therefore less likely to require medical care that could alert authorities to abuse. And even when they do sustain severe injuries requiring medical attention, they are less likely to be viewed as abused.

Adults often mistakenly perceive teenagers as deserving the abuse. The stereotypes of child abuse victims as small and helpless frequently leads to sympathy for very young victims of abuse and indifference to older victims. Abusers sometimes justify the greater use of violence against adolescents, due to their bigger size. Other people may expect teenage victims to be able to defend themselves against abuse. However, the dynamics of abuse are often more complex than that. Despite their physical strength, teens usually remain at the mercy of parents or other adults who wield greater power within the family.

Teenage Victims

Adolescence, roughly defined as the years between the ages of eleven and twenty, is generally a turbulent time marked by the onset of puberty, growth spurts, greater physical and mental abilities, and psychological changes. Parents often report being angry, frustrated, or confused about not being able to control their teenage children. As adolescents, people begin to forge their own identities, exploring new behaviors and asserting more independence, which frequently leads to disagreements and stress within the family. Wrongly blamed by abusers for "provoking" abuse, and lacking knowledge about family violence, teenage victims often think they deserve the abuse and do not seek help. Rather than going to child welfare authorities, doctors, or the police, adolescent victims sometimes end up in places like runaway centers.

In addition to physical injuries and emotional distress, teenagers who have been neglected or abused are at higher risk than nonabused teenagers for premature or risky sexual activity, pregnancy, suicide, alcohol or drug abuse, delinquency, school problems, eating disorders, and violence against siblings, peers, and parents. Self-destructive behavior and desperation caused by abuse can lead to other life-threatening problems like prostitution and exposure to HIV. Adolescents who are homeless, runaways, drug abusers, in prison, or pregnant are more likely to have experienced physical or sexual abuse than other teenagers.[28]

Because of these risks, abused adolescents often require special services such as crisis and drug counseling; education about sex, sexually transmitted diseases, and contraceptive use; legal and educational assistance; and help finding jobs and shelter. Overloaded social service agencies have traditionally focused on the needs of younger abused children, but recently more attention has been paid to the needs of abused teens. Some programs are specifically designed to help teens make the transition to independent living. In the final chapter, we will look at some of the efforts being made to help child and adolescent abuse victims. Now that we have a better idea of who may be at risk for abuse, let's examine who the abusers are and what factors are associated with abuse.

Who Are Child Abusers?

Who would hit an infant? Why would someone molest his niece, stepson, or grandchild? What kind of person routinely insults her own children?

Researchers of child abuse once assumed that people who abuse or neglect their children must be mentally ill or psychopathological. But more recent research has proved that most abusive parents are not clinically insane and that there are no set personality traits that lead to abuse.

However, surveys, clinical studies, and reports have theorized that certain personal and social factors may contribute to the likelihood of abuse. Although no single factor alone guarantees that abuse will occur, several factors together may increase the risk of child abuse.

As with other forms of family abuse, one of the most frequently cited risk factors is the abuser's previous abuse as a child. Since a significant number of child abusers experienced or witnessed abuse in their families as children, prior abuse is thought to increase the risk of becoming abusive. However, it is important to point out that the transmission of violence from one generation to the next is not inevitable and that most abused children do not become abusers themselves. Intervention can

39

Child Sexual Abusers

Child sexual abusers differ from other child abusers in one significant way—their gender. Research has shown that both men and women commit physical abuse, and some studies show that more mothers than fathers use physical violence against their children, perhaps due to the greater time they spend with them.[29] However, research indicates that most child sexual abuse is perpetrated by men.

About 90 to 97 percent of sexual abuse is committed by men.[30] Part of the discrepancy between the numbers of reported male and female offenders can be attributed to underreporting of women who sexually abuse children. Female sexual abusers are rarely identified due to the misconception that women cannot be sexual offenders. Women who sexually abuse children may be more likely to coax or verbally force victims to comply with abuse, rather than use physical force. This aspect may confuse victims, making it difficult for them to identify themselves as abused.

Whether male or female, people who commit sexual abuse against children are often respected, otherwise law-abiding citizens, who escape detection and prosecution by authorities. Usually, the abuser's first reaction to discovery is denial. He or she may act shocked, indignant, or angry, and try to minimize or distort what he or she did. The abuser may say that he or she accidentally touched the victim rather than admit to deliberate fondling. Other typical responses include: blaming the victim—saying that the victim seduced him or her; claiming mental illness; expressing regret and begging for another chance; threatening or trying to bribe the victim or other witnesses; violence; and self-destructive acts. In response to the abuser's denial or violence, other family members may blame the victim and put pressure on him or her to say that nothing actually happened. In the last chapter, we will discuss some of the things victims can do to get help in such crises.

prevent the repetition of maltreatment. For example, a person who was beaten by her mother as a child may gain support from other understanding adults who can help her overcome the effects of abuse and become a healthy adult and supportive parent.

Some studies have found that when maltreatment starts or occurs in adolescence rather than early childhood, the abusive parents are less likely to be victims of child abuse themselves and are often more open to treatment to stop the abuse.[31] Researchers believe that adolescent abuse frequently derives from another factor associated with child maltreatment: the parent's lack of knowledge about parenting.

Child rearing is a challenging process. Abusers often have lower tolerance for common actions by young children, such as crying, and they misinterpret their children's motivations. For example, an abusive mother may think that her son is deliberately trying to annoy her when he is actually just hungry or tired. Abusers may put unrealistic demands on their children and respond with rage when the child can't meet them. Teenage parents who are not ready for the demands of parenting may be particularly susceptible to becoming abusive for these reasons. Abusive parents with low self-esteem and poor coping skills often exhibit a need to control their children and view them as sources of gratification, rather than as independent persons who need nurturing and support.

Stressful situations such as financial pressures, poor housing conditions, marital conflict, and unemployment can also increase the risk of abuse. Parents may be over-whelmed and take out their frustration on children as vulnerable targets, rather than finding appropriate ways to express their feelings. The enormous difficulties and added stress produced by poverty may account for the higher incidence of reported child abuse among poorer people, although other factors may also account for this. (See discussion in Chapter 3, page 57–58.)

There has been much debate over the role of alcohol and drug abuse in child maltreatment. It is estimated that almost 10 million children and adolescents are affected in some way by their parents' substance abuse.[32] Alcoholics and other substance abusers are generally incapable of taking care of their children emotionally and physically and neglect their needs. The other parent may be preoccupied with looking after the substance-abusing parent and also neglect the children. In some cases, the child is forced to assume emotional and household responsibilities, because his or her parents' ability to do these things is impaired.

Substance abusers may also be at greater risk for physically, sexually, and emotionally abusing their children, since loss of control can lead to abuse. However, many experts emphasize that rather than being a cause of abuse, alcohol and drug misuse functions as an excuse for violence, abuse, and neglect.

Social isolation is another factor that increases the risk of child maltreatment. Abusing parents may feel isolated or keep themselves apart from friends, other family members, and their communities. Without physical and emotional support from other people, parents are more likely to feel frustrated and overwhelmed. And without the influence of outsiders telling them that abuse is wrong, abusers are less likely to change their behavior.

Cultural acceptance of violence and reluctance to

disturb family privacy also contribute to abuse. Physical abuse is sometimes excused as necessary punishment used to discipline children. Neighbors, teachers, and friends sometimes look the other way when they discover that a child is being mistreated because they do not want to pry into family matters. But the fact remains that child abuse and neglect are crimes that are punishable by law and since 1968, every state has mandated that professionals such as teachers, doctors, and social workers report abuses.

Perhaps the most consistently associated risk factor for child mistreatment is the existence of other forms of family abuse, particularly domestic violence. Unfortunately, many children are both victims of maltreatment and witnesses to abuse of a parent, sibling, or other family member. In the next chapter, we will discuss another form of abuse, domestic violence, and the impact it can have on people growing up in homes where it occurs.

The truth is that violence comes closer to many families than we would like to admit. Domestic violence is America's dark little secret.[1]

—Senator Bill Bradley

3

Domestic Violence

In October 1993, Representative Dan Burton, a Republican congressperson from Indiana, gave startling personal testimony in the House of Representatives about his experiences growing up in a violent home. While supporting a resolution to designate October as National Domestic Violence Awareness Month, he described what it was like to live with a father who savagely and regularly abused his mother.

> When I was about 5 years old I had a brother and sister who were both very small like myself, and I can remember my father attacking my mother and beating on her in the middle of the night. It is a terrible thing for a child to wake up at 1 o'clock in the morning hearing that kind of screaming and that violence, and your mother throwing a lamp through the window trying to get the attention of the neighbors so the

police will come. If there is anything we ought to be concerned with, it is child abuse and this kind of domestic violence, because it has a tremendous impact on young people for the rest of their lives.[2]

For nearly a decade, Burton's father, Charles, beat his mother, Bonnie. The almost weekly episodes of violence often began with verbal attacks and would escalate to his father battering his mother, sometimes ripping off her clothes or beating her to unconsciousness. In published interviews, Burton recalled the fear and sense of helplessness that he experienced as a child while witnessing his father's vicious behavior. He was also a victim of his father's severe beatings on more than one occasion, and he learned to avoid him as much as possible.

Over the years the battering became more severe and Burton's mother tried to leave his father several times. In 1950, she got a restraining order from the police and fled with the children to her mother's house, moving out permanently. Soon afterward, Burton's father broke into the house with a sawed-off shotgun and dragged her away. After several days, Burton's mother managed to escape from his father, who was arrested for kidnapping and jailed for two years. Burton's mother divorced his father and later married a kind and nonviolent man, who gave the family a safe and loving home.[3]

Unfortunately, cases of domestic violence such as this are not rare, and many of them do not end happily. The news is filled with tragic accounts of local incidents of domestic abuse and lurid celebrity cases that capture national attention. Every year, millions of women, like Burton's mother Bonnie, suffer from abuse perpetrated by their husbands, partners, or boyfriends. And every year, millions of children experience the trauma of witnessing the abuse of a parent.

Like child abuse, domestic violence is a widely under-reported crime. Due to the embarrassment associated with being a victim, pressures from family and society, and fear of retaliation, many victims do not report acts of domestic violence. In addition, most official government agencies do not specifically categorize domestic violence as a distinct crime in their records. Therefore, it is impossible to determine exact statistics on domestic violence. However, figures based on police and hospital reports, surveys, and studies indicate the pervasiveness of the problem.

It is estimated that over 3 to 4 million women are severely battered by a husband, boyfriend, or ex-partner each year.[4] According to the FBI, a woman is battered by her husband or boyfriend every fifteen seconds in the United States. Thirty to 50 percent of women in the United States will be physically abused by a husband or boyfriend at some point in their relationships. Every year, more than 3 million children witness domestic violence, and every year four thousand American women are battered to death by their spouses or boyfriends.[5]

The cost of domestic violence to both the individuals who suffer abuse and to society is enormous. Domestic violence is the leading single cause of injury to adult women in the United States—more than heart attacks, cancer, or strokes, according to the Surgeon General. According to the American Medical Association, about 35 percent of the women in hospital emergency rooms are there due to partner abuse. One third of the women in jail for murder have killed an abusive partner. And

ERWIN TRASK MEM. LIBRARY
PLAINVILLE HIGH SCHOOL

violent youths are four times more likely than nonviolent youths to come from homes where there is domestic violence.[6]

What exactly is domestic violence and why does it persist? In this chapter, we will discuss domestic violence as abuse within marriage, cohabiting, and dating relationships. Among other topics, we will look at the factors that may contribute to abuse, patterns of partner abuse, and stereotypes about victims and abusers. There will also be a section in this chapter on dating violence, which often affects teens and young adults.

What Is Domestic Violence?

"Violence is too soft a word. It is terrorism of the worst sort," noted Mark Wynn, a police sergeant and child witness of domestic violence.[7]

Domestic violence, partner abuse, and *battering* refer to abuse committed by one adult against another with whom the abuser has or has had an intimate or romantic relationship. These terms will be used interchangeably in this book. When the abuse involves people who are or who have been married, the term spousal abuse is sometimes used, although domestic violence often affects people who are not married.

Most domestic violence is committed by men against women. According to the Department of Justice, women are victims of domestic violence eleven times more often then men.[8] And although some sources suggest that women use violence against male intimates as frequently as men do against female partners, most evidence shows that the violence inflicted by men is much more severe.

48

Women who use violence often do so to defend themselves against an abusive partner. Since the majority of victims of this type of family abuse are women, victims of partner abuse will generally be referred to as female and abusers will be referred to as male in this book.

Domestic violence includes physical, sexual, and emotional acts of violence and abuse. Physical abuse usually involves the intent of causing harm or injury to the victim. It can take the form of slapping, punching, throwing the victim down or into walls and objects, tripping, biting, kicking, or twisting arms and legs. It may involve life-threatening behavior such as choking, stabbing, burning, attempting to drown, or shooting with a gun. Abuse may also refer to withholding necessary items, or to physical restraint such as locking the victim in a home or closet, handcuffing, or tying up a person. Sexual abuse includes genital mutilation and marital rape.

Psychological and verbal abuse is usually present along with physical or sexual abuse. It can involve behavior such as constant ridicule, accusations of infidelity or mental illness, threats against the victim or her loved ones, threatened suicide, harassment, and stalking. In most cases, domestic violence refers to physical as well as emotional abuse and it generally involves more than one act of physical harm.

The damage inflicted is often severe. According to the Department of Justice, if all domestic violence cases were reported, one third of them would be classified as felonies, the most serious type of crime. The other two thirds would be identified as simple assaults, with up to half of them involving serious bodily injury.[9] Not surprisingly, domestic violence can have harmful and long-lasting consequences on victims and their children.

The Impact of Partner Abuse on Victims

D.G., a university professor of women's studies and survivor of domestic violence, described the pain of experiencing partner abuse:

> I know how it happens, the wrenching love for the man who harms you, the man you've slept beside and lived with. I know the internalized guilt and shame, the fear it will happen again. I know the exhaustion of arguing with those who want to protect you. I know the humiliation of police indifference and contempt. I know that no one else can know what a woman going through this feels.[10]

Domestic violence causes more injuries to women than rape, muggings, and car accidents combined. Like child abuse victims, victims of partner abuse suffer from a wide range of physical traumas, such as bruises, loss of hearing or vision, and hypertension. Feeling desperate and trapped, some victims may respond to violence with violence against their abusers or may become suicidal. Murder of a victim or abuser is sometimes the endpoint of years of escalating violence that has gone unchecked. At least one third of the women murdered in the United States are killed by a husband or boyfriend.[11]

According to some research, pregnancy is a particularly dangerous time for battered women, and in some cases violence begins or intensifies during pregnancy. As many as one sixth to one third of pregnant women may be abused, according to some surveys.[12] Assaults during

50

pregnancy can cause rupture of the uterus, liver, or spleen; hemorrhaging; fetal fractures; birth defects; and pre-term labor that results in low-birth-weight babies.

Forced sex in marriage, or marital rape, may be the most prevalent type of sexual assault. Sexual assault is reported by 33 percent to 46 percent of female victims of physical partner abuse. Yet, sexual assault may be the most underreported and least prosecuted form of partner abuse, since many victims fear disbelief by outsiders.[13]

Women who have been abused by partners experience emotional pain as well as physical injuries. Like other people who are subjected to prolonged violence, they may develop a pattern of psychological reactions known as post-traumatic stress disorder. (See box on PTSD in Chapter 2, page 34.)

In addition to physical and emotional trauma, battered women often face indifference and discouragement from family, friends, and social institutions that refuse to help them or may even encourage them to stay in abusive situations. Attitudes that contribute to partner abuse will be discussed later in this chapter.

The Impact on Children Who Witness Domestic Violence

Rosemary Bray, the author of "Unafraid of the Dark," compared growing up in a home where her father battered her mother to living in a "suspended state of terror." She recalls hating her father's abuse of her mother, her mother's ineffective efforts to avoid "provoking" him, and her own fear of drawing his attention and anger.

Bray's experiences reflect those of many children growing up in homes where there is partner abuse.

> I can promise you that such children know the sound of every blow, the vibration of every wall as their mothers' bodies hit, the pitch of every voice raised in anger. I promise you that at least once, and probably more than once, those children lie crying in their beds, praying (if they have words for prayers), begging God or someone to make Mama and Daddy stop fighting, to make Daddy stop hitting, to make Mama stop crying. And if the beatings go on long enough, and no one helps and nothing changes, I promise you that they begin to make promises to themselves: I will never marry; I will never hit anybody, ever; I will never let anyone hit me, ever; I will never have children, so they will not have to live like this; when I have children, they will never hear this.[14]

Children growing up in homes where one parent batters the other may be fifteen times more likely to be abused or neglected than children from nonviolent homes. Some studies show that more than half of the battered women who are mothers and at least half of battering men who are fathers also beat their children.[15] Greater risk of neglect and abuse may also result from the fact that battered women are less able to care for and protect their children. Some battered spouses leave their children behind with the abuser, greatly increasing the risk of further harm to them.[16]

Children and adolescents who are not abused but who witness the abuse of a parent by another parent also suffer trauma. Although many parents believe that their children are not being exposed to battering, studies have concluded that most children living in violent homes observe the abuse inflicted by one parent against the other.[17]

Children are often traumatized by their fear for their mother's safety and their own sense of helplessness in protecting her. Some blame themselves for the abuse and try to intervene. Some, like President Bill Clinton, try to stand up to the batterer and defend their mothers against the abuse.[18] Many children are injured while trying to protect a parent. In one study of 146 adolescent children living in homes with partner abuse, all sons over the age of fourteen tried to protect their mothers and 62 percent were hurt in the process.[19]

Partner abuse may cause child witnesses to commit further destruction against people outside the family and themselves. Domestic violence is found in 20 to 40 percent of the families of chronically violent youths. Also, the children of abused mothers are six times more likely to attempt suicide and 50 percent more likely to abuse drugs or alcohol than children from nonviolent homes.[20]

Before examining the factors that can contribute to abuse, we will look at a frequently overlooked form of partner abuse: dating violence. A 1995 poll of young people found that 40 percent of girls between the ages of fourteen and seventeen said they had a friend their own age who had been hit or beaten by a boyfriend.[21]

Abuse between people who are dating and not married is not strictly a form of family abuse. However, it is a form of domestic violence that affects many teenagers and younger adults. The impact of abuse on young women may be even greater than it is on older adult women, who generally have greater financial and emotional resources than younger victims.

Dating Violence

On Saturday, May 30, 1992, shots rang out on a street in Boston when twenty-one-year-old art student Kristin Lardner was shot to death by her ex-boyfriend, Michael Cartier. After shooting Lardner three times in the face and the head, Cartier returned to his apartment and killed himself with the same gun.

At the time of the murder, Cartier, a twenty-two-year-old European-American bouncer, was under court order to stay away from Lardner, who had obtained a permanent restraining order against him for beating and stalking her. Kristin Lardner was a promising, outgoing college student in a fine arts program run by the School of the Museum of Fine Arts and Tufts University. She had dated Michael Cartier for a few months during the spring of 1992, after meeting him in January at a Boston nightclub. Although things started smoothly, it was only a short time before Lardner knew something was wrong.

Irrationally jealous and suspicious of Lardner's male friends and wildly unpredictable, Cartier first hit her after they had been going out for about two months. After hitting her, he broke down crying and apologizing. Although shocked and injured, Lardner accepted his apologies and continued to see him for a few more weeks. However, soon afterward in mid-April, Cartier assaulted her following an argument, throwing her down on a sidewalk a few blocks from her apartment and kicking her repeatedly in the head and legs. Lardner managed to escape and make it home safely with the help of passing motorists who witnessed the assault. Following that incident, Lardner broke off the relationship and refused to see Cartier again. Unwilling to accept the end of the relationship, Cartier started calling Lardner up to eleven times a day while trying to intimidate her into not contacting the police.

In mid-May, Lardner decided to turn to the legal system for help and filed a police complaint charging Cartier with assault and battery, larceny, intimidation of a witness, and violation of the domestic abuse law. She also obtained a restraining order against Cartier, which specified that he avoid all contact with her, but the court order did little to protect her. Due to a series of bureaucratic errors, Cartier was not arrested at the time of the hearing for the restraining order. After the hearing he was as free as he had been before it. A week and half after the order was issued he killed Lardner.

Lardner's tragic story focused attention on the dangers and problems of dating violence when her father George Lardner, Jr., a *Washington Post* reporter, investigated it and wrote a Pulitzer Prize-winning article about it.[22] Abuse between people who are dating or living together is a common form of domestic violence. According to some surveys, about one in three females will experience violence inflicted by their boyfriends before they reach adulthood.[23]

In most ways, dating violence resembles spousal abuse. For example, the patterns of abuse and the increased danger at the time of separation from the batterer are the same whether the victim is dating, living with, or married to the abuser. And as the Kristin Lardner case shows, the abuse can be just as lethal in dating situations as it is within marriage.

However, dating violence differs from spousal abuse in that people who are dating or living together, but are not married, usually do not have the joint legal and financial relations that married people do. In addition, dating violence is generally not taken as seriously as spousal abuse is by most people. According to surveys, young men are more likely to admit that they hit their girlfriends than older men are to admit to abusing their wives. In one study of college students, male students said their main motives for committing violence against a girlfriend were a desire to "intimidate," "frighten," or "force the other person to do something." Male students also frequently reported that they used violence in response to sexual denial. When dating violence involves teenagers, adults may minimize the seriousness of the verbal and physical abuse that occurs.

The rate of sexual assaults, including date rape, of young women by men they are dating is very high. Adolescents and young adult women are more at risk for rape by an acquaintance or someone they are dating than by a stranger. And the overall rates of rape victimization are highest among females sixteen to nineteen years old. In one survey of college students, 42 percent of the women reported experiencing some type of sexual assault. Reports of both sexual and nonsexual physical abuse of females in dating or cohabiting situations have increased over the last two decades.[24]

Whether the abuser is a husband, a boyfriend, or another type of romantic partner, the underlying causes and patterns of abuse are the same. In the next few sections, we will look at the factors and patterns associated with domestic violence.

Causes of Domestic Violence

What causes a person to abuse his or her partner? What factors put a person at risk for being a victim of domestic violence? What life conditions enable or encourage this activity?

People who study and work with victims and abusers have many theories about what factors are often associated with partner abuse. However, these theories vary and sometimes contradict one another. For example, some sources state that risk factors for abuse include: unemployment, lack of education, poverty, youth, pregnancy, isolation, alcohol and drug abuse, and abusive family background. Yet other studies note that the relationship of alcohol and drug abuse to domestic violence is unclear and that most batterers and victims did not grow up in homes that they considered violent.[25]

Another controversial issue is whether partner abuse is more common among people with lower incomes. According to official records, domestic violence appears to be more prevalent among lower income groups than in higher income groups. Some studies note that the stress caused by poverty and the lack of alternative resources for dealing with crises may account for the higher prevalence of abuse among lower-income people. However, other researchers point out that victims with lower income are more likely to get help from public agencies like battered women's shelters and hospital emergency rooms than wealthier victims who have access to more private sources of help. They conclude that poorer victims are simply more likely to be counted in official statistics than more affluent victims.[26] Also, although factors such as poverty and substance abuse may be linked with battering, most people who experience those problems do not perpetrate abuse. Therefore, other factors must account for why battering occurs.

In looking at the factors that contribute to abuse, we may wonder about the personality traits and psychological characteristics of the people involved. This leads to the question: who is likely to become a victim or perpetrator of partner abuse?

Who Are the Victims? As with other forms of family abuse, one of the most commonly held misconceptions is that domestic violence only occurs among poor, uneducated people and only in certain ethnic and racial groups. The truth is that battering occurs in all socioeconomic levels and within all religious, geographic, age, racial, and ethnic groups in the United States.

Since partner abuse affects such a broad spectrum of people, it is impossible to determine typical characteristics of domestic violence victims and abusers. Abuse survivors and batterers may be rich, middle-class, or poor; may be European-American, African-American, Asian-American, Latino, or Native American; may live in rural areas or cities; and may be straight, gay, or bisexual. They may be engineers, doctors, construction workers, lawyers, police officers, musicians, or teachers. There is no evidence that people who experience domestic abuse are generally mentally ill. As one researcher put it, a woman's risk of being battered "has little to do with her and everything to do with who she marries or dates."[27]

Who Are the Abusers? While some studies hypothesize that physiological factors such as head injuries may contribute to abusive behavior, most focus on psychological and behavioral traits found among abusers. They note that batterers often have low self-esteem, are pathologically jealous, lack communication skills, and have limited coping abilities and extreme reactions to stress.[28] Remarks or comments that would not be perceived as significant to other men are often interpreted as insults or challenges by abusive men. (See chart on Risk Factors for Partner Abuse, page 61.)

One factor that all abusers may have in common is their need to control their victims and families at any cost. Many studies have concluded that abusers are more likely to have grown up in homes where there was domestic violence than in nonviolent homes, and that these batterers, who may have been victims of abuse as children, have learned that violence is an effective means of getting what they want. Other researchers point out that the message that abuse is an appropriate method for maintaining power over another person is reinforced by a society that does little to discourage this type of behavior.[29]

Partner abuse can be seen as part of a generalized violence against women in a culture that has low respect for women. Although domestic violence is a crime, society tends to look the other way and excuse abuse when it consists of a man beating his wife or girlfriend, even in high-profile celebrity cases. Former football star O. J. Simpson retained his contracts as a spokesperson for Hertz and as an on-air analyst for NBC after pleading "no contest" and being sentenced for spousal abuse of his now deceased wife, Nicole Brown Simpson, in 1989.[30]

59

Many experts state that domestic violence occurs because men learn that it is acceptable and do not learn nonviolent means they could use to express frustration, anger, or other feelings. As Robert L. Allen and Paul Kivel, who work with the Oakland Men's Project, a non-profit group devoted to eliminating male violence, racism, and homophobia, put it:

> Men batter because we have been trained to; because there are few social sanctions against it; because we live in a society where the exploitation of people with less social and personal power is acceptable. In a patriarchal society, boys are taught to accept violence as a manly response to real or imagined threats, but they get little training in negotiating intimate relationships. And all too many men believe that they have the right to control or expect certain behavior from "their" women and children; many view difficulties in family relationships as a threat to their manhood, and they respond with violence.[31]

Batterers often try to deny or minimize the severity of their violence and blame the victims for the abuse. "They all come in thinking she's the problem, that she made him do it," noted Gail Pincus, who runs a program for batterers.[32]

A wide belief that domestic abuse is acceptable can enforce the batterer's notion that he can get away with abusive behavior. Some of the widespread attitudes toward battering illustrate how society encourages abuse.

Attitudes Toward Domestic Violence

Today, domestic violence is illegal in every state. However, bias against battering victims is revealed by the fact that in some states battering is a misdemeanor—a

Risk Factors for Partner Abuse

Many sources cite previous experiences growing up with domestic violence as the highest risk factor for future abuse. Here is a list of risk factors compiled by sociologists:[33]

- Male saw father hit mother
- Male unemployed
- Male uses illicit drugs at least once a year
- Male and female have different religious backgrounds
- Total family income is below the poverty line
- Male is between eighteen and thirty years of age
- Male did not graduate from high school
- Male has blue-collar occupation, if employed
- Male or female uses severe violence toward children in the home
- Male and female live together and are not married

less serious crime—whereas the same acts committed by a stranger are considered felonies, or more serious crimes.

Some cities spend more on their zoos than their states spend on helping victims of domestic violence. Both individuals and institutions often look the other way, refusing to help victims even when battering occurs right in front of them. "Every time something happened, it was in public, and nobody stopped to help," noted Rose Ryan, a survivor of dating violence, in reference to assaults she suffered.[34]

People sometimes hesitate to intervene in partner abuse cases because they maintain an idea that what occurs between intimate partners is a private matter. Some people believe that both partners are equally accountable for the abuse and that victims somehow provoke abusers into using violence.[35] Often, people blame the victim for not leaving or improving the situation. The stereotype persists that strong women leave their abusers and only weak, masochistic, or passive women are victims of abuse. This viewpoint overlooks the fact that the only person responsible for the abuse is the abuser and it does not take into account the many obstacles and difficulties that women who are in abusive situations face when they are trying to leave. In order to understand some of these difficulties, we need to look at patterns of abuse and the phenomenon of separation violence.

Patterns of Partner Abuse

In most cases, abuse worsens over time, becoming more severe and more frequent. Some researchers and people who work with battered women have noted a cycle of three phases in domestic violence cases. During the first phase, tension builds and a series of relatively minor verbal and physical abuse incidents occur. In the second phase, there is an acute battering incident in which the victim suffers severe violence from the abuser. Police and others are most likely to be alerted to the abuse during this phase. The acute battering incident is often followed by the third phase—a period of calm, in which the abuser tries to woo the victim back with apologies, gifts, and promises to never repeat the abuse. However, in most abusive relationships, the batterer goes back on his promise and the cycle of abuse recurs.[36]

As the level of violence and abuse escalates over the course of a relationship, the victim may respond with attempts to end the relationship. The point of separation, however, is usually the most dangerous time for the victim.

Separation Violence. The single greatest motive given in a sample of mate homicides in the city of Jacksonville, Florida, from 1980 to 1986 was the offender's refusal to accept the termination of the relationship.[37] Although many people assume that a battered woman will be safe after she leaves the abuser, this is generally not the case. Abuse may continue after separation for up to two thirds of all battered women, and battering often intensifies after separation. According to the Department of Justice, up to 75 percent of domestic assaults reported to law enforcement agencies occur after the partners have separated. And battered women are 75 percent more likely to be killed at and after the point of separation.[38]

Often, batterers respond to a victim's attempts to move out of a shared residence, or terminate a relationship, with anger and fear. Many abusers are dependent on their victims and the victim's leaving may arouse feelings of intense jealousy and a sense that it is intolerable for the victim to be independent or involved with another person. Batterers often feel threatened by the loss of control over the victim's life that the end of the relationship represents.

Faced with future separation, abusers may threaten to hunt down and kill victims, and they may stalk and harass them for years after a divorce or breakup. Restraining orders and orders of protection obtained from the police to keep batterers away from victims are often ineffective. Unless the abuser is arrested and jailed, many battered women face continuing and worsening abuse after they have terminated their relationships. In a typical pattern of abuse, women are killed after years of battering, stalking, and their effort to leave.[39]

Why Victims Stay and When They Leave

"It's typical that we focus on a woman's irrationality, asking 'Why didn't she leave?' but not 'Why did he hurt her?,' "[40] observed the writer Annie Gottlieb.

Perhaps the most frequently asked question regarding partner abuse is: Why does she stay? Although this may not be a fair question given the fact that the abuser and not the victim is responsible for perpetuating the abuse, the answers to the question illustrate aspects of domestic violence.

Although some form of abuse, such as verbal ridicule, is often present from the start, most women do not enter relationships that are physically violent at the onset. Violence generally starts slowly and infrequently and escalates over time. Once a woman finds herself in an abusive situation many factors may keep her from leaving.

First, the danger of leaving accounts for why many women stay in abusive situations. Since stalking and battering often continue or escalate after separation, many women fear that leaving will not stop and may intensify the abuse. Victims may also develop survival skills that focus on minimizing the risk of danger and just making it through the day, rather than planning escape. Emotional bonds with the abusive partner, the victim's physical and mental exhaustion, or a belief that she deserves the abuse or is helpless to change the situation are also factors that keep women from leaving.

Successful and safe separation requires resources that many battered women cannot access easily. Some researchers theorize that women who have few resources, receive discouraging responses from professionals such as police officers, and maintain a traditional viewpoint about the roles of women are more likely to stay in abusive situations than women in different situations.

The victim may be financially dependent on the abuser and may have no means of supporting herself and her children. Women are generally paid less than men. Also, half of all married women with children don't work outside the home and have no separate income.[41]

Immigrant battered women sometimes face additional obstacles such as language barriers when trying to get help from the police or social service agencies. Some battered women have been sponsored for residency or legal immigration by their husbands, who threaten to divorce and deport them if they try to leave.

Battered women in rural areas often live far from the nearest battered women's shelter and may be geographically isolated from other sources of help. Although battering occurs at equal rates among gay and straight people, battered lesbians and gay men face homophobia and more difficulties getting shelter, restraining orders, and other help from service providers who may not take their complaints as seriously as those of heterosexual women.[42]

Victims usually make several attempts to leave before permanently separating from their partners. Women may try to leave when they can no longer hide the abuse; their financial situation improves; their children grow up; they fear for their children's safety; or when neighbors, doctors, or others recognize and report the abuse.[43] The intervention and support of family, friends, neighbors, and professionals are often essential to helping individual battered women find safety.

Over the last twenty-five years, as services for battered women have expanded and public attention has focused on the problem, prevailing attitudes about domestic violence have changed dramatically. In the final chapter, we will examine how different institutions have responded to partner abuse and what you can do to help eliminate the problem.

Although child maltreatment and partner abuse are the best-known forms of family abuse, other forms of abuse are also widespread. In the next chapter, we will discuss three other forms of abuse: elder abuse, parent abuse, and sibling abuse.

Violence has reached epidemic proportions as a public health problem in America. It takes many forms and affects Americans at every age and every stage of life.[1]

—Former Surgeon General Antonia C. Novello

4

Other Forms of Family Abuse

In March 1992, an eighty-two-year-old man named John Kingery was found abandoned near a restroom at a dog-racing track in Post Falls, Idaho. An employee of the racetrack found him sitting alone in a wheelchair, holding a bag of diapers, and wearing a sweatsuit, bedroom slippers, and a baseball cap imprinted with the words, "Proud to be American." Because Mr. Kingery suffered from Alzheimer's disease and could not remember his name, officials had trouble identifying him at first. All the labels and identifying marks had been removed from his clothing and the wheelchair, except for a note which said that he was an Alzheimer's patient named "John King" who required twenty-four-hour care. However, he was soon identified by the administrators of a nursing home in Portland, Oregon, who recognized a photograph of him released to the media. After the mystery of his identity was solved, he was flown home to Portland. Officials investigating the case focused on Mr. Kingery's daughter, Sue Gifford, who had checked him out of the nursing home about ten hours prior to the time he was discovered at the racetrack.

Elder Abuse

John Kingery's case and others like his have drawn attention to the growing problem of abandonment of ailing, elderly people by younger family members. Sometimes called "granny dumping," abandonment is a form of elder abuse that has become more widespread over the last fifteen years. According to the American Association for Retired Persons, an elderly person is abandoned every day in a hospital emergency room in the United States, usually by his or her child. A survey of 169 hospitals conducted by the American College of Emergency Physicians found that seventy thousand elderly patients were abandoned by a family member or caregiver in 1991.[2]

Like other family members, elders such as parents or grandparents are susceptible to mistreatment by those they depend on for their physical or emotional well-being. Elder abuse is the mistreatment of an elderly person by a spouse, sibling, child, or friend. Until recently, knowledge about elder abuse was hindered by disbelief, misinformation, and lack of research. However, as the population of elderly persons in the United States continues to grow, more and more attention is being paid to problems they face.

More than one hundred forty thousand cases of

suspected elder abuse are reported yearly. As with child abuse and domestic violence, the number of reported cases represents only a fraction of what experts believe are the actual rates of mistreatment, and estimates of the actual number of cases of elder abuse vary widely. Most researchers project that between 1 and 2.5 million Americans over the age of sixty, or about 2.5 to 5 percent of the older population, suffers mistreatment. Over two thirds of elder abuse is thought to be perpetrated by children, spouses, or other relatives.[3]

Elderly relatives may suffer from the same types of physical, sexual, and emotional abuse that younger family members do. In addition to the examples of physical abuse noted in previous chapters, physical elder abuse may include forced feeding, overmedicating with tranquilizers or other medicines, and positioning a person with a disability incorrectly.

In recent years, many states have passed laws that make elder neglect a crime. Neglect of an elderly family member occurs when someone who has assumed responsibility for the elderly person's well-being fails to respond adequately to his or her needs. These needs include food, shelter, clothing, emotional support, freedom from harassment and violence, and the other requirements of daily life. Some authorities make a distinction between active and passive neglect of elderly relatives, based on the caregiver's motives. *Passive neglect* is defined as the unintentional failure to fulfill a caregiver's obligation, which occurs when there is no willful attempt to hurt the person. *Active neglect* involves the intentional failure to provide necessary things and a deliberate attempt to hurt the older person physically or emotionally. Abandonment of an older relative falls under this category. Other actions such as depriving the person of eyeglasses, hearing aids, or dentures; failing to take her or him to medical appointments; and denying food are also considered active neglect.

Financial or *material abuse* is another form of elder abuse that has become much more widespread over the last decade. The elderly may be victims of financial exploitation more than any other form of elder abuse. Financial exploitation is the illegal, unethical, or improper use of the elderly person's funds, property, or other assets gotten through force or trickery. Examples of financial exploitation include stealing money or possessions, forcing the person to sign a check or contract, and tricking someone into changing his or her will.

Late-onset spousal abuse is sometimes associated with changes related to the aging process such as retirement or physical conditions like strokes and Alzheimer's disease. These diseases may cause personality changes and lowered inhibitions. Because elderly people frequently are frail and vulnerable to health problems, any form of mistreatment can result in dangerous or life-threatening conditions. Physical abuse is not necessarily more severe than neglect or psychological abuse.

Causes of Elder Abuse

Passive neglect, which is probably the most widespread form of elder abuse, generally occurs when well-meaning family members assume responsibility for an older person and then cannot meet that person's needs. Caregivers in such situations may find themselves unexpectedly burdened by long-term physical, emotional, and financial costs that become overwhelming. To avoid passive neglect, families need to carefully consider their resources when thinking about providing care for an aged relative who can no longer live on her or his own.

There is some evidence that people taking care of relatives who are severely dependent due to disabling health problems are more likely to become abusive or violent. This is especially true when the elderly person has become violent due to the disorder. Alzheimer's disease is the most common cause of severe dependency. Alzheimer's is a condition associated with aging that causes the person who has it to suffer changes in memory, thought, personality, language, and physical functions. People with Alzheimer's generally become more and more incapacitated over a long period of time. Other causes of severe dependency include stroke, cardiovascular diseases, and fractures. Without professional help, few families are capable of caring adequately for a person who is severely dependent.[4]

Any elderly person, regardless of health status, sex, race, ethnicity, or socioeconomic group, may be at risk for elder mistreatment. Although experts debate the role of many factors in contributing to abuse, some commonly cited risk factors are listed in the chart on page 72.

Like other victims of family violence, mistreated elderly people may go unnoticed by medical or social service professionals who don't believe that a person could be abused by his or her relative. People the victim knows may fear embarrassing him or her by bringing up the subject. The same stereotypes and misinformation that

71

Factors That May Contribute to the Risk of Elder Abuse

- Victim and offender reside together
- Offender's dependence on the victim
- Victim's dependence on the offender
- History of mental illness in offender or victim
- Alcohol or drug abuse by victim or offender
- Victim socially isolated from others
- Recent stressful life events in the family, such as unemployment
- Victim's physical or mental impairment
- Previous family abuse or neglect

thwarted recognition of child abuse and domestic violence have held back society's response to elder abuse.

Over the next thirty years, the number of Americans over the age of eighty-five is expected to increase five times to 15 million, and the number of people with Alzheimer's is expected to triple to 12 million by the year 2020.[5] With the population getting older and cutbacks in government funding to social service programs increasing, elder abuse is becoming a growing problem. The growth of the elderly population, however, has increased public concern about elder abuse and it is the form of "hidden" mistreatment that is the best known. Two other forms of family abuse, parent abuse and sibling abuse, remain more obscure.

Parent Abuse

The idea of children abusing their parents seems absurd or impossible to many people. Because of their greater physical strength, size, and authority within the family, parents are thought to be immune to violence and abuse from their children. Unfortunately, this is not always the case.

Although estimates for the occurrence of parent abuse fall far below the rates of child mistreatment, they remain significant. According to most research, 5 to 12 percent of children abuse their parents. One study, conducted in 1982, found that 9 percent of parents, or 2.5 million, reported at least one act of violence from a child between the ages of ten and seventeen living at home. According to the same survey, about 3 percent of parents, or nine hundred thousand, reported being subjected to severe forms of violence including kicking, punching, biting, beating up, or use of a gun or knife. Also, between 1977 and 1986, the murder of a parent or stepparent by a child occurred almost daily in the United States, with more than three hundred parents killed per year.[6]

Several factors tend to obscure the fact that parent abuse occurs. Since children and young adolescents are much smaller and physically weaker than their parents, they are considered incapable of inflicting harm against an adult. However, even small children can cause severe injury to their parents.

Moreover, most, if not all, societies dictate that

73

children love and obey their parents, and people generally react with horror when parents are victimized by their offspring. Parents who are abused often have difficulty reporting the abuse, because it seems to be so unusual. Like victims of elder abuse—who are sometimes simply older victims of parent abuse—mistreated parents may feel ashamed or may fear that they will be considered responsible for their children's actions.

Some researchers have concluded that children who commit parent abuse are usually between the ages of thirteen and twenty-four, although younger children are known to attack and even kill parents. Sons are slightly more likely to be violent or abusive than daughters, especially as they get older. There is conflicting research about whether mothers or fathers are more likely to be victims.[7]

The occurrence of parent abuse is sometimes associated with the existence of other forms of abuse within a family. Children and teenagers who witness or experience violence are more likely to become abusive toward their parents than youths who do not. This may be particularly true of children who commit parricide.

Parricide, a term used to refer to the murder of a parent by his or her child, represents an extreme form of parent abuse. Between 1977 and 1986, around sixty-five birth parents were killed by adolescents each year. Perpetrators of parricide are typically European-American males, and many are under eighteen years old.[8]

According to researchers, most adolescents who commit parricide are severely abused themselves, with some sources reporting that more than 90 percent were abused by their parents. Teenagers are more likely to commit parricide than adults in abusive situations, because they generally lack income, other homes to go to, and the emotional resources that adults have. Murder, however, is a crime that should be avoided despite the horror of an abusive home. Children and adolescents who feel trapped in abusive situations need to know that they have options available to them other than killing the abuser. As Kathleen M. Heide, author of *Why Kids Kill Parents*, put it, "Abused and neglected children who are aware that they can get help would be less likely to conclude that killing the abusive parent is the only solution."[9] In the final chapter, we will look at some of the options available to victims of family abuse.

Sibling Abuse

Sibling abuse, or abuse between brothers and sisters, is both the most widespread and the most overlooked form of family abuse. It is in fact so commonplace that it is accepted as normal by most people. Most parents tend to assume that "kids will be kids" and do not take notice when their children hit, insult, or beat up each other. Many parents believe that it is important for children to learn how to deal with aggressive conflicts. They think fighting among siblings is preparation for fighting peers.

Widespread acceptance of violence among siblings clouds the recognition of sibling abuse as a serious problem. There have been only a handful of studies on this type of family abuse, but the ones that have been conducted reveal the pervasiveness of the problem. In a national study on family violence conducted in 1980, researchers found that more than four fifths (36.3 million) of children age three to seventeen committed at

75

least one violent act toward a sibling living at home in one year.[10]

According to parent reports, the children in the 1980 study averaged twenty-one acts of violence per year, with 42 percent kicking, biting, or punching; 16 percent beating up; 40 percent hitting with an object; 0.8 percent threatening to use a gun or knife; and 0.3 percent using a gun or knife. The sociologists who conducted the study estimated that over 19 million children use severe violence against a sibling each year. In a 1990 survey of adolescents age sixteen to nineteen, more than 60 percent of the teenagers reported being either a victim or perpetrator of sibling violence during the year prior to the study.[11]

Both boys and girls commit sibling violence. In the 1980 family violence study, 83 percent of boys and 74 percent of girls were found to use physical aggression toward a sibling. Girls were found to be less violent than boys at all ages, but the difference was small.[12] Families with only boys, however, generally have more sibling violence than families with only girls.[13] Although rates of teenage sibling violence remain high, children have been found to use violence less frequently to resolve conflicts as they grow older. This may be because they develop verbal skills or because they spend less time with each other as they pursue interests outside the home.

Children and adolescents are also subjected to sexual abuse committed by their siblings. Like physical sibling abuse, sibling incest is the least researched but possibly the most common form of family sexual abuse. It is estimated to occur five times more often than parent-child incest. While some researchers see sexual acts

76

between siblings as generally harmless or part of acceptable sexual play and exploration, there is growing concern about sibling sexual abuse that can cause victims to suffer from lowered self-esteem, sexual problems as adults, and becoming victims of sexual abuse later.[14]

One recent study of sibling incest offenders found that the sexual abuse was often severe. The severity of abuse was revealed by factors such as a significant age gap between perpetrators and victims, the recurrence of incidents and long duration of abuse, a high incidence of oral sex and vaginal penetration, and the frequent use of verbal threats to maintain secrecy about the abuse. Researchers conclude that most sibling incest is not reported and that even when it is reported to parents, the abuse often continues because parents deny or minimize the significance of abusive behaviors.[15]

Since so few studies have been conducted, little is known about the causes of all types of sibling abuse. Brothers and sisters may attack each other because they are smaller, weaker targets than parents or other adults who make them feel powerless. Physical, emotional, and sexual sibling abuse is often learned from abusive adults. Although many abused children are very protective of their younger brothers and sisters, some may learn and repeat harmful actions. Studies of sibling incest have found that a significant number of child and teenage offenders have experienced physical abuse, sexual abuse, or both from an adult family member.

Researchers note that siblings generally have enormous influence on each other as they grow up. Sibling abuse has been linked to poor peer relationships in the victim and other behavioral problems in the aggressor. The effects of sibling sexual abuse may resemble post-traumatic stress disorder (see page 34) and other consequences of child sexual abuse.[16]

Perhaps even more than with other forms of family abuse, prevention of sibling abuse depends on the elimination of the idea that it is acceptable. The expansion of services to prevent abusive family patterns in general would help lessen sibling abuse. In the next chapter, we will discuss how different institutions have responded to family abuse and highlight some of the efforts that aim at preventing and intervening in abusive family situations.

For every change we need to make, someone in the country not only already knows how to do it, but is doing it successfully.[1]

—Ann Jones, coauthor of *When Love Goes Wrong*

5

Society's Role: Responding to Abuse Within Families

Child abuse survivor Seriya Stone emphasized that people need to know that alternatives to family violence exist:

> I think at this point the biggest thing is still for people who are suffering in relationships to have the courage and the faith that there is a life beyond the situation. A lot of people they just can't see it, can't see anything but what's happening and they stay. The focus needs to be upon those people who are not happy to hear a voice that's telling them you need to do something else.[2]

Despite the appearance of an increase in levels of family abuse, researchers believe that life in the United States today is more humane, with children exposed to less family violence and neglect, than at any other time in history.[3] Both the appearance of greater violence and the actual decline in abuse may result from greater public awareness and less tolerance of family abuse. As we look more closely at some of the ways family abuse is being addressed today, it is important to remember how public responses can help or hurt victims of mistreatment. In the next few sections we will look at how various parts of society—the police, the legal system, social services, medical professionals, and the media—have responded to abuse within families.

Mandatory Reporting

One of the most important changes in the last three decades has been the establishment of mandatory reporting laws regarding child abuse and neglect. Every state requires that certain professionals who suspect a child is being mistreated must report the suspected mistreatment to the police or the state or local agency that investigates child mistreatment cases. Professionals who are legally obligated to report suspected abuse include teachers, medical professionals, and law enforcement officers. In many states, not only professionals but anyone—including neighbors, friends, and other relatives—who suspects abuse or neglect must report their suspicions under state law. People who fail to report suspected abuse can be fined or imprisoned, have their professional licenses revoked, or be sued for liability damages.

Mandatory reporting laws apply to child and adolescent victims of suspected abuse or neglect by relatives and nonfamily members. Every state has a Child Protective Services office, which receives and oversees investigation of all reports of suspected mistreatment. Most states also have a toll-free, 800 telephone number to call to make reports, which can be made anonymously. You don't need to have evidence or be absolutely certain to make a report, since cases are investigated to find out what is going on and reports are confidential.

If the Child Protective Services office finds that a child's safety is being jeopardized by sexual or physical abuse, the child may be removed from the home and placed in temporary shelter or foster care. In most child neglect cases where the child is not in immediate danger, caseworkers try to help the family improve the situation without removing the child from the home.

Mandatory reporting laws regarding elder abuse vary from state to state. During the 1980s, many states established laws, based on child abuse legislation, to require the reporting of elder abuse. In 1992, forty-three states required doctors and other health and social service workers to report suspicions of elder abuse. (The other seven states had voluntary reporting systems in place.)[4] However, people working with elder abuse victims later came to see the early emphasis on mandatory reporting as a mistake. Adult victims of abuse, including the elderly, differ from children in their ability to make decisions about their lives and provide for themselves materially. Many people maintain that reporting abuse usually should be left to the adult who is experiencing it. This remains a controversial area. Some professionals point out that a person who is experiencing abuse may not be able to act in his or her best interest because of threats or fear. They believe that sometimes intervention is needed to help the victim obtain safety, even when intervention is not initially welcomed.

Unlike legislation concerning elder abuse and child

abuse, few states require the reporting of partner abuse to protective agencies. Mandatory reporting is not thought to help battered women, who need to determine the safest course of action for themselves. However, since violent and sexual assault are crimes, professionals are often required to report abusive actions to law enforcement.

Whether or not mistreatment is reported, it is important for people who come into contact with victims to be aware of the situation. It is especially important for professionals to recognize family abuse so that they can spot life-threatening situations and provide help to the best of their ability. Medical professionals are one group of people who have tried to improve their responses to family violence in recent years.

Medical Responses to Family Abuse

Because abused children, battered women, and other mistreated adults frequently need to seek medical attention, doctors, nurses, and other medical professionals are often in a position to detect family abuse. As the American Medical Association's guidelines for identifying and treating elder abuse state, "A physician may be the only person outside the family who sees the older adult on a regular basis, and he or she is uniquely qualified to order confirmatory diagnostic tests such as blood tests or X rays, to recommend hospital admission, or to authorize services, such as home health care."[5]

However, like other groups of people, doctors have traditionally been reluctant to recognize and react to signs of abuse that they see. For example, although it is estimated that 35 percent of the women who go to hospital emergency rooms are there due to partner abuse, only 5 percent of these domestic violence cases are identified as such.[6] Studies of doctors have revealed that misconceptions about family abuse often keep them from recognizing it.

In one survey, physicians said that exploring the possibility of abuse among patients was like "opening a can of worms or Pandora's box," because it could unleash overwhelming problems. Many doctors also find it hard to believe that someone they know or a person who is similar to them could experience or perpetrate abuse. Some are more likely to diagnose domestic violence or child abuse among poor or nonwhite patients.[7]

Recently, however, the American Medical Association (AMA) and other organizations have stressed the need for physicians to commit time to addressing abuse. They note that failing to diagnose abuse can lead to inappropriate and even harmful treatments. When only the symptoms of abuse are treated without recognition of family violence, abuse may continue and victims may feel that there's no one to turn to. One study found that about one fifth of battered women seeking treatment had received medical attention for abuse-related injuries eleven times before.[8] And since violence often escalates over time, physicians can intervene in situations before they become life threatening.

In October 1991, the AMA introduced its Physicians' Campaign Against Family Violence to help doctors recognize family violence as a disease requiring medical attention. In 1992, the AMA published guidelines to help doctors identify and treat abuse of the elderly, children, and intimate partners.

Many medical researchers have recommended that doctors routinely screen for family abuse during patient visits. As with other health-related phenomena once considered too embarrassing to discuss, such as smoking and drug use, the awkwardness associated with discussing abuse would be reduced if it was talked about as a part of regular visits. For both victims and witnesses of family violence, simply talking about their experiences with a sympathetic professional can provide the relief that enables them to take further action.

Several Surgeons General, the AMA, and others have called for physicians to become educated about the dynamics of abuse. They should know how to make reports and referrals to social services and be willing to work with other community professionals to improve services to victims. The U.S. Public Health Service has developed guidelines to help communities implement programs to prevent violence. Hospital-based programs that coordinate several different departments have been found to be particularly effective. New York City's Mount Sinai Medical Center runs a model program in which the geriatrics department, social work services, and nursing department work together to address elder abuse. The program provides training, case consultations, direct clinical services, and resource material for health-care professionals.

In the course of treatment, medical workers may document abuse by keeping accurate records, having photographs taken, or confirming sexual abuse through medical exams. Often, this documentation later becomes an essential part of the law enforcement process.

Police and Legal System Responses

Sometimes, the first contact victims have with outsiders is not with medical professionals, but with the police and the legal system. This is most frequently true in domestic violence cases, which are generally reported to local law enforcement precincts rather than to protective services.

Partner abuse cases represent the largest single category of calls to the police. Yet police response to domestic violence has been traditionally marked by ineffectiveness. Many studies have found that police officers responding to domestic violence calls often do not file reports and fail to arrest abusers. One study conducted in Washington, D.C., in 1989 reported that the police did not arrest the abusers in 85 percent of partner abuse incidents in which the victims were found bleeding from wounds.[9]

Police officers may fail to carry out standard arrest procedures if they think of domestic violence as a private matter. Rather than arresting a person who has assaulted his partner, an officer may try to "cool off" the situation, simply warn the offender, or refer the couple to social services. Such procedures ignore the victim's constitutional right to protection and can further endanger her by reinforcing the idea that no one will help her and by allowing violence to continue.

Sometimes police officers are reluctant to arrest batterers because of the unpredictable outcome of domestic cases. Victims often refuse to press charges or later drop charges against batterers because of fear of retaliation, mistrust or lack of information about the justice system, and loyalty to the abuser. Even when this does not happen, prosecutors often refuse to prosecute abuse cases, further discouraging initial police intervention.

Since the likelihood of winning a conviction of the accused person is an important factor to prosecutors, they may refuse to proceed with domestic violence cases because of the difficulty of successful prosecution. Often there are no other witnesses to the violence except the children, who may be frightened into not testifying. Prosecution is generally a long and time-consuming process. Thus, the victim may later drop charges because the abuser has intimidated her over time. In some cases that have made it to trial, judges have refused to convict the abuser because they misunderstand or tolerate battering.

When police officers fail to arrest batterers and prosecutors refuse to proceed with cases, offenders may be encouraged to believe that they can get away with committing violence. "Society needs to recognize it as a crime and hold the abusive person accountable for his actions, which means arrest and jail time, but that doesn't always happen," said Diane Crosson, training and technical assistance specialist at the Texas Council on Family Violence.[10]

The arrest and prosecution of perpetrators who commit criminal acts is generally considered an important part of intervention with all forms of family abuse. Researchers and people working with victims of child abuse, elder abuse, and domestic violence emphasize the need for such protection, especially since many abusers will not stop the abuse unless they are arrested and jailed. Arrest and prosecution can also give victims the time to organize, leave the abusive situation, and get help from social service and legal experts.

Mandatory Arrest and Innovative Programs

Battered women's advocates have recommended that police develop clear procedures for domestic violence calls, file reports even when arrests are not made, and use arrest as a preferred response. To overcome the special obstacles victims face, many states and cities now require police officers to arrest suspected abusers in domestic calls if there is any visible sign of assault or if they have reason to believe assault occurred, even when victims refuse to press charges. This policy, which is called mandatory arrest, was adopted by twenty-five states in 1994.[11]

Many battered women's groups, however, do not support the new mandatory arrest laws. They state that studies of mandatory arrest have revealed contradictory results, reducing violence in some cases but increasing it in others. Not arresting a batterer may be more dangerous to the victim in the short term, but arresting him may make things worse for the victim when he is released from jail.[12] In some areas, mandatory arrest policies have resulted in increased numbers of dual arrests of both the victim and the abuser. Opponents of mandatory arrest say that arrest should be the preferred but not obligatory response, used at the discretion of the police officer.

Several programs that coordinate law enforcement and social services have been recognized for their effectiveness. The Domestic Abuse Intervention Project of Duluth, Minnesota, works with a local battered women's coalition to help victims secure safety through protection orders, shelters, and the legal system. Police officers are trained to view domestic violence as a crime, use mandatory arrest and consistent procedures, and advise victims about shelters. Prosecutors are discouraged from throwing out charges and judges are advised to sentence guilty offenders consistently.

Some districts use a method called victimless prosecution to address the fact that battered women may be intimidated into dropping charges. San Diego County pioneered this policy, which allows cases to be prosecuted whether or not the victim presses charges, using evidence from 911 calls, photographs, medical and police records, and testimony from neighbors or other witnesses.

Law enforcement also can help victims of family abuse by evicting an abuser from the home, prohibiting him from having contact with the victim, ordering abusers to attend counseling or alcohol and drug treatment programs, awarding custody of children to a nonabusing parent, and requiring guilty offenders to pay for expenses related to assault. To help victims move through the legal process, many police departments and social service organizations have established victim advocacy programs.

Victim advocates can provide emotional reassurance, facilitate communication between the victim and prosecutors, contact shelters, help explain the legal process, file legal forms, and help develop a plan for long-term safety. Advocates can also help victims of partner, elder, and child abuse obtain restraining or protection orders that prohibit the abuser from having contact with the victim. More than fifty thousand women in the United States seek restraining or protection orders each month.[13]

Going through the legal process can be particularly

confusing and upsetting for a young person. A child's credibility may be attacked in court by defense attorneys. And although the victim's testimony is usually crucial to successful prosecution, children and teenagers often fear testifying and speaking to authorities about abuse, particularly sexual abuse. Children's Advocacy Centers (CACs) have been established throughout the United States to make child abuse investigation more effective and less intimidating for child victims. CACs coordinate the responses of law enforcement, child protective services, and medical and mental health services to minimize the trauma of the investigation process.

Protective Laws

Many new laws and legal reforms also have been established to better protect people from family abuse. For example, in 1989 the state of Texas passed a law that made neglect of an elderly person a prosecutable offense. The law states that anyone who accepts responsibility for taking care of a person over sixty-four, a child, or an invalid must provide adequate care for that person.[14]

In 1993, more than five hundred bills concerning partner abuse were introduced in state legislatures.[15] Since 1990, every state has passed antistalking laws that prohibit people from continually harassing and threatening victims and give police the authority to issue protective orders before violence is repeated. In August 1994, Congress passed and President Bill Clinton signed the Violence Against Women Act (VAWA) as part of an anticrime bill. VAWA designated $1.6 billion for prevention and education programs, including funding for battered women's shelters and training of police, prosecutors, and judges to improve handling of partner abuse cases. Through a historic civil rights provision, the act also enables victims of gender-biased crimes such as rape and sexual assault to sue the offender in civil court for financial compensation.

Innovative programs and the enactment of recent laws have greatly strengthened law enforcement's response to family abuse. However, prosecuting offenders is just one part of the intervention process. Another important aspect is the help that social services can provide.

Social Services Responses

Medical professionals, victim advocates, and police officers who first come into contact with family abuse victims often refer them to social service providers for additional longer-term assistance. Social service professionals, like psychologists, social workers, and group counselors, can help protect victims from further harm and help them regain a sense of control over their lives.

Social service professionals may provide prosecutors with information and in some cases testify on behalf of the victim in court. Social service professionals can also help victims find permanent housing or temporary shelter. Today there are about fifteen hundred battered women's shelters in the United States. These shelters provide temporary housing for battered women and their children, usually allowing women to stay for up to thirty days.[16]

To relieve parental or caregiver stress in child and

elder mistreatment situations, protective service workers can bring in home health aides or professional homemakers to help take care of the child, elder, or household needs. In some cases, protective services can pay for child or adult day care, so the caregiver gets a break from having to provide constant supervision. When unemployment is a factor, social services can help the victim or offender find employment.

In addition to this kind of practical help, social service professionals can help victims recover emotionally from abuse. Experts emphasize the need for victims of family abuse to receive therapeutic treatment as soon as they can. Therapists who are trained to treat children and adult survivors of mistreatment can help them recover from harmful psychological effects by addressing feelings of anger, depression, fear, shame, and worthlessness. Since many victims blame themselves for the abuse, therapists can help them learn that they were not responsible for it. As Judith Cornelius, clinical director of the Travis County Children's Advocacy Center stated, "It's very important for a child to be helped to make sense of what happened to them. They need to feel that they are believed and that they are not at fault. They need to have the ability to know that they have not been damaged in any way."[17]

Intervention for Abusers

Experts also recommend therapeutic intervention accompanied by legal action for abusers. Child sexual abusers need long-term psychological treatment. Most perpetrators will deny the abuse even when confronted and will continue to abuse children if they are left untreated. Through intensive, long-term therapy, an abuser may be able to develop better understanding of the harmful consequences of his or her actions and learn to change his or her behavior. Since perpetrators resist changing and usually keep abusing the child unless they're strictly monitored, legal charges usually must be brought against them to keep them away from the child.

At least two hundred social service agencies provide group counseling led by a trained male counselor for partner batterers. Although no treatment method has been found that consistently changes batterers, group therapy may be more effective than individual counseling. Some experts state that couples' counseling can be dangerous for the victim, because it can perpetuate the idea that the victim is somehow responsible for the abuse. However, other experts assert that couples' counseling can be helpful and in some cases may be the best solution.[18]

Many batterer treatment programs have been developed around the idea that batterers need to hear from other men that violence toward women is unacceptable. In one pioneering treatment program called Emerge in Cambridge, Massachusetts, abusers undergo individual therapy followed by a nine- to twelve-month group counseling program. Batterers learn to confront their excuses for violence and to change sexist beliefs by giving each other criticism and support under the guidance of a counselor. Attendance and completion of the program is enforced by legal penalties.

Limitations in Services

Like other segments of society, social services have come under fire for not always responding to family abuse as well as they could. Following tragedies like the Elisa Izquierdo case, the child welfare system has been criticized for promoting a policy of keeping families together, even when the child is in a life-threatening situation.

Part of the problem is that lack of funding has created overburdened systems that cannot help everyone in need. Although the number of shelters has grown tremendously over the last twenty-five years, there still are not enough to accommodate the demand. One study conducted in Boston in 1990 found that for every two women with children admitted to shelters, five women and eight children had to be turned away due to limited space.[19]

"There is nowhere near the amount of money we need to be real effective," said Char Bateman, a policy specialist with Child Protective Services in Texas. "We pretty much provide services only to those people who are at highest risk. Our workloads are always unmanageable. We would be able to provide more prevention and intervention resources if there were more money devoted to services for people."[20]

It is clear that despite vast improvements, medical, law enforcement, and social service workers will never be able to help everyone who suffers from family abuse after it has been committed. Experts in these fields consistently conclude that society needs to focus more intently on preventing abuse before it happens.

Education to Prevent Family Abuse

"People lack information and education about what it is and what can be done. Not only the people living in it, but also the communities need to recognize the problem and commit resources to amending it,"[21] said Diane Crosson, a training and technical assistance specialist for the Texas Council on Family Violence.

In an ideal world, all cases of family abuse would be prevented before they began. In an effort to achieve this goal, numerous educational programs have been developed over the last few decades.

One way in which child abuse and neglect can be prevented is through education in parenting skills. Being a parent can be a very challenging process, requiring skills that do not come naturally. Parenting skills classes can teach people how to raise children safely by managing households better, improving communication skills, controlling anger, and disciplining without violence. Char Bateman noted, "With physical abuse and neglect, it's sometimes just ignorance. The parents may think the only way to discipline a child is through severe beating, so a parenting skills class and just learning can help."[22]

New parents and especially teenage parents who lack knowledge about living skills and face special stresses may benefit the most from these courses. Some high schools have adopted parenting skills courses to help teenage parents.

Educational programs have also been developed to help children recognize abuse and get help if they are being mistreated. These programs are important because the earlier abuse is recognized, the earlier it can be stopped. Many people first realize that they have been abused, and seek help, in college, when the subject is discussed in class or on campus.

Sometimes child sexual abuse can be avoided if the child learns that abuse is wrong and illegal, but OK to talk about. Groups such as Illusion Theater of Minneapolis and Child Assault Prevention of Columbus, Ohio, go to schools and conduct workshops teaching children about the differences between appropriate affection and abusive touching. Using humorous skits, role playing, films, puppets, and coloring books, they emphasize that children have the right to control their bodies, to not have people touch them in ways that are uncomfortable, and to say "no" to abusers. The groups also teach children how to get out of dangerous situations by yelling or telling an adult.

Many experts also emphasize the need to educate children growing up in homes with parents who are abusing alcohol or drugs because of the risk of abuse. The number of children under the age of eighteen whose parents are alcoholics is estimated to be about 7 million.[23] Through schools, youths can learn about groups like Alateen, which help teenagers cope with problems caused by their parents' substance abuse.

Other in-school programs aim at preventing domestic violence. Since 1987, the Women's Center and Shelter of Greater Pittsburgh has run "Violence Free—Healthy Choices for Kids," which teaches fourth- and fifth-graders how to resolve conflicts without using violence, provides support groups for children and parents, and informs teachers about how to spot children who may be living with family violence. The center also runs three-day Dating Violence Prevention Programs, in which older students participate in discussions and role-playing to learn about the differences between abusive and healthy relationships.

Teaching elderly people about how to plan to reduce the risk of abuse can prevent some forms of mistreatment. For example, a senior citizen can choose a trusted family member or friend to help manage resources and find supportive care in advance, in case he or she later becomes incapable of doing these things due to illness.

Educating Through the Media

Various forms of media such as television, newspapers, magazines, and radio have also helped educate the public about family abuse. Although media coverage of family abuse has been criticized for reinforcing stereotypes, organizations and celebrities have also used the media to increase public understanding. During the mid-1970s, public service advertisements using slogans such as "Child abuse hurts us all" broadcasted the message that child abuse and neglect are widespread problems.[24] More recent efforts have informed people about where to go for help and how to help prevent different forms of family abuse.

In September 1992, three major networks and the public television network aired a one-hour documentary on child abuse called *Scared Silent: Exposing and Ending Child Abuse*. Hosted by talk-show host, producer, and abuse survivor Oprah Winfrey, the documentary focused on six true stories of physical, sexual, and emotional abuse, interviewing both perpetrators and victims. The show, which was seen by 50 million viewers, publicized and boosted calls to child abuse hotlines.[25]

Wide media coverage of sensational cases like the O. J. Simpson trials have also had the positive outcome of raising public awareness of family abuse and available services. In the weeks following the murder of Nicole Brown Simpson, calls to domestic violence hotlines increased by as much as 80 percent in some places. Stories following the murder that focused on O. J. Simpson's history of battering Nicole Brown Simpson also spurred tougher laws in many states.[26]

In 1994, the Family Violence Prevention Fund (FUND) produced a television spot that urged people who overhear or witness domestic violence to report it. The spot aired as part of the first national public education campaign to end partner abuse, called "There Is No Excuse for Domestic Violence."

George Lardner, Jr.'s Pulitzer Prize-winning article about the murder of his daughter Kristin brought attention to the problems in the way the justice system handles domestic violence cases (see Chapter 3). Lardner's article helped to spur the establishment of the first computerized statewide Domestic Violence Registry, which improves the effectiveness of tracking and prosecuting batterers.

Many professional athletes, actors, and other celebrities have also spoken publicly about their experiences with family abuse to help people understand its devastating impact. In October 1994, several Miami Dolphins football players participated in a panel discussion on partner abuse. Recalling personal experiences, they urged men to respect women and learn alternatives to violence. "If you're gonna be committed to someone, be able to talk to them," said fullback James Saxon. "You don't have to hit someone to make a point."[27]

Many believe that media attention has helped change public attitudes toward family abuse. A 1990 survey reported that 90 percent of the public said that they believed yelling and swearing at children can result in long-term emotional problems. And in a study conducted by FUND in 1993, 87 percent of Americans said that battering by husbands or boyfriends is a serious problem and 81 percent thought something could be done to end partner abuse.[28]

Again and again, experts note that public intolerance of family abuse is the key to both prevention and intervention. And as we have seen, people in many situations can have a great impact on the way family abuse is handled in day-to-day life. Friends, neighbors, and anyone in contact with victims can do several things to help them.

What You Can Do and Where to Go for Help

If you know someone who is being abused by a family member, boyfriend, or girlfriend, you can help by showing that you appreciate the complexity and difficulty of his or her situation. It's good to let the person know that you believe what he or she tells you about the situation, that you want her or him to be safe, and that you're willing to help. Wendy Varnell, a coordinator at Pathways, a child mental health center, has this advice for teens who know someone in an abusive situation:

> They should encourage the person to tell an adult about the abuse and emphasize that this isn't right or safe. They should also recognize that it took a lot for that person to tell them and they might be very

surprised. Often the abuse is guarded so well that the peer never suspects it. The person who discloses the abuse might also be mad, because of all the things they're experiencing and they need to know that it's OK to be mad and that they've done the right thing by telling. A peer or friend should say that you should tell an adult and encourage them to do it themselves. If they absolutely refuse to, the peer needs to do it themselves, but they should tell the person, so they're not just a passive victim again.[29]

Usually the adults who can be most helpful in these situations are guidance counselors, teachers, or other people who are professionally trained to handle disclosures of mistreatment. Whether you are a friend of a victim or someone experiencing abuse yourself, it is best to go to an adult you really trust. Experts warn that a family member may not necessarily be the best person to go to. "I wouldn't suggest talking to a family member, because a lot of times, the most loyal family member cannot deal with it. They can't deal with it because if they could deal with it, they'd be dealing with it," said Seriya Stone.[30] If the first person you speak to does not believe you or give you the support you need, keep telling other people until you find someone who does.

If you want to make a report to authorities directly you can call your local police station, the local Child Protective Services, or the child welfare department number listed under "Child Abuse" or "Children Services" in the Yellow Pages or in the front of the phone book. You can also ask the operator for assistance by dialing 911 or 0. Most states have toll-free 800 numbers for reporting. You can also call the national toll-free child abuse hotline at 1-800-4-A CHILD (1-800-422-4453). When giving a report, you may be asked to give the victim's name, address, and a description of what is happening.

If you know someone living with partner abuse or another form of family abuse, it is good to tell them that you care about their safety and to encourage them to tell an adult who can help. If you need to notify people yourself, you can call the police station, find helpful numbers listed in the phone book under "Crisis Intervention Services," "Social Service Organizations," "Health Agencies," or "Hotline Numbers for Community Services," or call the national domestic violence hotline at 1-800-799-SAFE (7233). If you are aware of a battering occurring, it is best to call 911 immediately for help.

If someone is mistreating you or you feel someone may have abused you, remember that you are not alone and that millions of people grow up with family abuse and survive it. There are lots of people and services to help you. Any group that works with teenagers probably knows about family abuse and most schools will have information about what kind of help is available locally. You can also call the national helpline numbers or use the on-line resources listed in the back of this book. The helplines offer crisis counseling and can direct you to local resources. The most important thing is to start telling people whom you trust, so you can begin to make changes and get help.

If you are interested in helping survivors and preventing family abuse from happening, many options are available to you. Any group that works with people depends on volunteers. Many organizations that help teenagers focus on peer support and train young volunteers to do peer counseling, answer hotline calls, and provide other resources to people who need it.

You can tell your local, state, and national elected officials that you support strong laws against family abuse by writing, calling, or e-mailing them. You can e-mail most government officials, including the president, to express your opinions about different issues.

Students can also get involved in sending out the message that family abuse is not acceptable by organizing discussions, writing articles in the school newspaper, or making information about where to turn to for help more available in their schools. Since schools are the places where young people are most likely to find assistance first, you may want to ask teachers or school administrators about how to bring more educational programs and professionals who work on family abuse to your school. You can also start a group for students who have experienced family abuse.

Statistically, chances are that you know someone who has experienced a form of family abuse or neglect. The devastating effects of mistreatment within families and the costs we pay in further violence and destruction are well documented. By using your voice as a caring friend or a concerned member of society, you can help make our families and communities safer for everyone.

Where to Find Help

Helplines

If you are witnessing or experiencing a family abuse emergency, it's best to call 911 for immediate help. However, you can also call the following toll-free helplines, which provide crisis counseling and referral to local resources.

Boystown National Hotline
1-800-448-3000

Covenant House Hotline
1-800-999-9999

Elder Care Locater
1-800-677-1116

National Child Abuse Hotline
1-800-4-A-CHILD (1-800-422-4453)
Text Telephone: 1-800-222-4453
Offers services in more than one hundred languages

National Domestic Violence Hotline
1-800-799-SAFE (7233)
Text Telephone: 1-800-787-3224
Offers services in more than one hundred languages

National Family Violence Helpline
1-800-222-2000

Organizations

For more information about family abuse issues and resources, you can call or write to the following organizations:

Al-Anon/Alateen
1600 Corporate Landing Pkwy.
Virginia Beach, VA 23454-5617
1-800-344-2666

American Association for Retired Persons
601 E St., NW
Washington, D.C. 20049
1-800-424-3410

Childhelp U.S.A.
P.O. Box 630
Los Angeles, CA 90028
1-800-422-4453

Family Violence Prevention Fund
383 Rhode Island St., Suite 304
San Francisco, CA 94103-5133
415-252-8900

**National Center on Child Abuse
and Neglect Clearinghouse**
P.O. Box 1182
Washington, D.C. 20013
1-800-394-3366

National Committee for the Prevention of Child Abuse
332 S. Michigan Ave., Suite 1600
Chicago, IL 60604
1-800-835-2671

National Council on Child Abuse & Family Violence
1155 Connecticut Ave. N.W., Suite 400
Washington, D.C. 20036
1-800-222-2000 or 202-429-6695

National Resource Center on Child Abuse and Neglect
63 Inverness Drive East
Englewood, CO 80112
1-800-227-5242

National Resource Center on Child Sexual Abuse
107 Lincoln St.
Huntsville, AL 35801
1-800-543-7006

National Resource Center on Domestic Violence
6400 Flank Dr., Suite 1300
Harrisburg, PA 17112-2778
1-800-537-2238

Parents Anonymous
675 W. Foothill Blvd., Suite 220
Claremont, CA 91711
909-621-6184

On-line Resources

The Internet is a good place to look for more information about family abuse resources and issues. Newsgroups, listservs, Internet Relay Chat rooms (IRCs), and Multi-User Domains (MUDs) provide forums for discussing abuse. Also, numerous World Wide Web pages list and have links to abuse information.

World Wide Web Pages:

Abuse Survivors' Resources
http://www.tezcat.com/~tina/psych.shtml

Child Abuse Resources
http://idealist.com/wounded_healer/car.shtml

Family Violence Prevention Fund
http://www.igc.apc.org/fund/

Mental HealthNet: Self-Help Resources Abuse
http://www.cmhc.com/guide/abuse.htm

**Mental HealthNet: Self-Help Resources
Domestic Violence**
http://www.cmhc.com/guide/domest.htm

SafetyNet: Domestic Violence Resources
http://www.cybergrrl.com/dv.html

The Survivor's Page
http://cam043212.student.utwento.nl/

Yahoo! Domestic Violence: Organizations
http://www.yahoo.com/Society_and_Culture/Crime/Crimes/
Domestic_Violence/Organizations/

Newsgroups:

alt.abuse.offender.recovery
alt.abuse.recovery
alt.abuse.transcendence
alt.sexual.abuse.recovery
alt.support.abuse-partners
alt.support.dissociation
alt.support.trauma-ptsd

IRCs:

#aat
#abuse&healing

MUD:

telnet://psicorps.org:3333

Listserv:

Survival-Domestic Violence List
send subscription request via e-mail to:
majordomo@facteur.std.com

Chapter Notes

Chapter 1

1. Barbara Ehrenreich, "Oh, *Those* Family Values," *Time*, July 18, 1994, p. 62.

2. Marc Peyser with Carla Power, "The Death of Little Elisa," *Newsweek*, December 11, 1995, p. 42.

3. David Van Biema, "Abandoned to Her Fate; Neighbors, Teachers and the Authorities All Knew Elisa Izquierdo Was Being Abused. But Somehow Nobody Managed to Stop It," *Time*, December 11, 1995, p. 32.

4. Lizette Alvarez, "Stepfather Is Indicted in Elisa's Case," *The New York Times*, January 26, 1996, p. B6; Nina Bernstein, "As Abuse Case Details Emerge, a Memo Harshly Assails Agency," *The New York Times*, December 5, 1995, p. A1; Dianne Metzger, "A Child Dies, and the System Tries to Hide Everyone's Problem," [Letter to the Editor], *The New York Times*, December 3, 1995, p. 14; "Questions on a Child's Death," *The New York Times*, December 3, 1995, p. 2.

5. Beverly Merz, "Family Violence and the Physician," *American Medical News*, January 6, 1992, p. 3.

6. Javad H. Kashani, Anasseril E. Daniel, Alison C. Dandoy, and William R. Holcomb, "Family Violence: Impact on Children," *Journal of the American Academy of Child and Adolescent Psychiatry*, March 1992, p. 181; Robert E. Emery, "Family Violence," *American Psychologist*, February 1989, p. 321.

7. *Facts About Child Abuse and Neglect*, National Council on Child Abuse & Family Violence, Washington, D.C.: undated, p. 1; "Facts About Family Violence and Hospitals," *Hospitals*, November 5, 1992, p. 25.

8. "Violence Begins at Home," *The New York Times*, July 5, 1994, p. A16; James O. Mason, M.D., DrPH, "The Dimensions of Family Violence," *Public Health Reports*, January/February 1993, pp. 1–3.

9. "Facts About Family Violence and Hospitals," p. 25; Antonia C. Novello, Mark Rosenberg, Linda Saltzman, and John Shosky, "From the Surgeon General, US Public Health Service," *JAMA*, June 17, 1992, p. 3132; Mason, pp. 1–3; Joseph R. Biden, "Domestic Violence: A Crime Not a Quarrel," *Trial*, June 1993, p. 56.

10. Mary Lystad, "Interdisciplinary Perspectives on Family Violence: An Overview," *Violence in the Home: Interdisciplinary Perspectives*, ed. Mary Lystad (New York: Brunner/Mazel Publishers, 1986), p. xi; Suzanne K. Steinmetz, "The Violent Family," *Violence in the Home: Interdisciplinary Perspectives*, p. 53.

11. Kashani et al., p. 181.

12. Steinmetz, p. 53.

13. Lystad, pp. xi–xii; Julia Hamilton, "Child Abuse and Family Violence," *The Violent Family: Victimization of Women, Children and Elders*, ed. Nancy Hutchings (New York: Human Sciences Press, 1988), pp. 90–91.

14. Nancy Hutchings, *The Violent Family: Victimization of Women, Children and Elders*, p. 15.

15. Daniel Glaser, "Violence in the Society," *Violence in the Home: Interdisciplinary Perspectives*, p. 6.

Chapter 2

1. Donna E. Shalala, excerpt from a speech given at the Tenth National Conference on Child Abuse and Neglect, *NRCCSA News*, January/February 1994, p. 1.

2. Personal interview with Seriya Stone, January 19, 1996.

3. Ibid.

4. Ibid.

5. Ibid.

6. "Facts About Child Abuse and Neglect," National Council on Child Abuse & Family Violence, Washington, D.C., p. 1.

7. Karen McCurdy and Deborah Daro, *Current Trends in Child Abuse Reporting and Fatalities: The Results of the 1993 Annual Fifty State Survey* (Chicago: National Committee to Prevent Child Abuse, 1994), pp. 3, 6, 11, 14.

8. Javad H. Kashani, Anasseril E. Daniel, Alison C. Dandoy, and William R. Holcomb, "Family Violence: Impact on Children," *Journal of the American Academy of Child and Adolescent Psychiatry*, March 1992, p. 183.

9. Beverly Merz, "Family Violence and the Physician," *American Medical News*, January 6, 1992, p. 3; Julia Hamilton, "Child Abuse and Family Violence," *The Violent Family: Victimization of Women, Children and Elders*, ed. Nancy Hutchings (New York: Human Sciences Press, 1988), pp. 92–93.

10. Tamar Lewin, "Two Polls Find Wide Abuse of Children," *The Austin American-Statesman*, December 7, 1995, pp. A1, A10.

11. Jane Marks, "We Have a Problem," *Parents*, March 1990, p. 66.

12. Ibid., pp. 63–67.

13. James A. Monteleone, Sheila Glaze, and Karen M. Bly, "Sexual Abuse: An Overview," *Child Maltreatment: A Clinical Guide and Reference*, ed. James A. Monteleone and Armand E. Broeder (St. Louis: G.W. Medical Publishing, Inc., 1994), p. 115.

14. David Finkelhor, "Current Information on the Scope and Nature of Child Sexual Abuse," *The Future of Children*, Summer/Fall 1994, pp. 31–32; Kathleen M. Heide, *Why Kids Kill Parents: Child Abuse and Adolescent Homicide* (Columbus, Ohio: Ohio State University Press, 1992), pp. 22–23.

15. Finkelhor, p. 31.

16. Ibid., p. 32.

17. Frank Sabatino, "50 Million People Watch Child Abuse Documentary," *Hospitals*, November 5, 1992, p. 28.

18. "Postnatal Causes of Developmental Disabilities in Children Aged 3–10 Years—Atlanta, Georgia, 1991," U.S. *Centers for Disease Control Morbidity and Mortality Weekly Report*, February 16, 1996, p. 130.

19. Becky Bradway, "Just the Facts . . . Child Sexual Abuse," *Coalition Commentary* (Springfield, Ill.: Illinois Coalition Against Sexual Assault, Summer 1993), p. 7.

20. Monteleone et al., p. 126.

21. Personal interview with Wendy Varnell, January 11, 1996.

22. Personal interview with Judith Cornelius, January 26, 1996.

23. David Finkelhor, "Prevention Approaches to Child Sexual Abuse," *Violence in the Home: Interdisciplinary Perspectives,* ed. Mary Lystad (New York: Brunner/Mazel Publishers, 1986), p. 298.

24. Council on Scientific Affairs, American Medical Association, "Adolescents as Victims of Family Violence," *JAMA,* October 20, 1993, p. 1852; Bradway, p. 6; Finkelhor, "Prevention Approaches to Child Sexual Abuse," p. 297.

25. Personal interview with Wendy Varnell, January 11, 1996.

26. "Adolescents as Victims of Family Violence," pp. 1851–1852.

27. Teri Randall, "Adolescents May Experience Home, School Abuse: Their Future Draws Researchers' Concern," *JAMA,* June 17, 1992, p. 3127.

28. "Adolescents as Victims of Family Violence," p. 1854.

29. Richard J. Gelles and Claire Pedrick Cornell, *Intimate Violence in Families,* 2nd ed. (Newbury Park, Calif.: Sage Publications, 1990), pp. 56–57.

30. Monteleone et al., p. 115.

31. "Adolescents as Victims of Family Violence," p. 1853.

32. *Child Abuse and Neglect Fact Sheet* (Washington, D.C.: National Clearinghouse on Child Abuse and Neglect Information.)

Chapter 3

1. Bill Bradley, "We Can't Hide Domestic Violence," *Philadelphia Inquirer,* September 26, 1994, p. A11.

2. "National Domestic Violence Awareness Month," *Congressional Record,* October 26, 1993, p. H8485.

3. Dan Burton, "When Violence Hits Home," *People,* April 4, 1994, pp. 91–96.

4. Estimates vary greatly, ranging between 2 million and 28 million victims of domestic violence per year. The most widely cited statistics, however, state that more than 3 to 4 million women a year are victims of domestic violence. *Statistics Packet,* 3rd ed. (Philadelphia, Penn.: National Clearinghouse for the Defense of Battered Women, 1994), pp. 90–93.

5. "National Domestic Violence Awareness Month," p. H8485; Ira Berkow, "Is Sports on Trial with O.J.?" *The New York Times,* July 7, 1994, p. B9.

6. Joseph R. Biden, "Domestic Violence: A Crime, Not a Quarrel," *Trial,* June 1993, p. 56; Antonia C. Novello, Mark Rosenberg, Linda Saltzman, and John Shosky, "From the Surgeon General, US Public Health Service," *JAMA,* June 17, 1992, p. 3132; Michele Ingrassia and Melinda Beck, "Patterns of Abuse," *Newsweek,* July 4, 1994, p. 28; "Violence Begins at Home," *The New York Times,* July 5, 1994, p. A16.

7. George Lardner, Jr., "Judges' Conference Hears of Family 'Terrorism,'" *The Washington Post,* April 4, 1993, p. A20.

8. Ingrassia and Beck, p. 26.

9. Biden, p. 56.

10. D.G., "What's Love Got to Do with It?" *Ms.,* September/October 1994, p. 34.

11. Bradley, p. A11; Biden, p. 56.

12. Ingrassia and Beck, p. 28.

13. Suzanne K. Steinmetz, "The Violent Family," *Violence in the Home: Interdisciplinary Perspectives,* ed. Mary Lystad (New York: Brunner/Mazel Publishers, 1986), p. 58; Council on Scientific Affairs, American Medical Association, "Violence Against Women: Relevance for Medical Practitioners," *JAMA,* June 17, 1992, p. 3187.

14. Rosemary L. Bray, "Remember the Children," *Ms.,* September/October 1994, pp. 39–40.

15. Biden, p. 56; Bray, pp. 42–43; "Children of Domestic Violence: Risks and Remedies," *Child Protective Services Quarterly,* Winter 1992, p. 1.

16. *Courts and Communities: Confronting Violence in the Family* (San Francisco: State Justice Institute Conference, March 25–28, 1993), p. 27; Kathleen M. Heide, *Why Kids Kill Parents: Child Abuse and Adolescent Homicide* (Columbus, Ohio: Ohio State University Press, 1992), p. 103.

17. "Children of Domestic Violence: Risks and Remedies," p. 2.

18. David Maraniss, *First in His Class: A Biography of Bill Clinton* (New York: Simon & Schuster, 1995), pp. 34–41.

19. Bray, pp. 42–43.

20. *Courts and Communities: Confronting Violence in the Family*, p. 28; Bray, pp. 42–43.

21. Tamar Lewin, "Two Polls Find Wide Abuse of Children," *Austin American-Statesman*, December 7, 1995, p. A1.

22. David Ellis, "Bloody Obsessions; For Many Stalking Victims, Threats Are a Prelude to Murderous Violence," *People*, May 17, 1993, p. 71; George Lardner, Jr., "The Stalking of Kristin; The Law Made It Easy for My Daughter's Killer," *The Washington Post*, November 22, 1992, p. C1.

23. S. Kuehl, "Legal Remedies for Teen Dating Violence," in *Dating Violence: Young Women in Danger*, ed. Barrie Levy (Seattle: Seal Press, 1991).

24. "Violence Against Women: Relevance for Medical Practitioners," pp. 3184, 3187.

25. Ingrassia and Beck, p. 28; Margaret Martin, "Battered Women," *The Violent Family: Victimization of Women, Children and Elders*, ed. Nancy Hutchings (New York: Human Sciences Press, 1988), pp. 73–75.

26. *Answers to Some Commonly Asked Questions About Domestic Violence*, Domestic Violence Fact Sheets, National Woman Abuse Prevention Project (undated).

27. Martin, pp. 73–75; Ingrassia and Beck, p. 29.

28. Jill Smolowe, "When Violence Hits Home," *Time*, July 1, 1994; America Online: LonStr 75. May 29, 1995; Martin, pp. 73–75.

29. State of Iowa, *Final Report of the Supreme Court Task Force on Courts' and Communities' Response to Domestic Abuse*, submitted to the Supreme Court of Iowa, August 1994, p. 8.

30. Sara Rimer, "Handling of 1989 Wife-Beating Case Was a 'Terrible Joke,' Prosecutor Says," *The New York Times*, July 18, 1994, p. 10; Anna Quindlen, "Remember Nicole Simpson," *The New York Times*, June 22, 1994, p. A21.

31. Robert L. Allen and Paul Kivel, "Men Changing Men," *Ms.*, September/October 1994, p. 50.

32. Quindlen, p. A21.

33. Richard J. Gelles, Regina Lackner, and Glenn D. Wolfner, "Risk-Markers of Men Who Batter, A 1994 Analysis," *Newsweek*, July 4, 1994, p. 29.

34. Biden, pp. 56, 58; Ingrassia and Beck, p. 28; Lardner, p. C1.

35. Gloria Jacobs, "Where Do We Go From Here: An Interview with Ann Jones," *Ms.*, September/October 1994, pp. 60–61.

36. Kashani et al., p. 184; Lenore E. A. Walker, "Psychological Causes of Family Violence," *Violence in the Home: Interdisciplinary Perspectives*, pp. 78–79.

37. Christine E. Rasche, "'Given' Reasons for Violence in Intimate Relationships," *Homicide: The Victim/Offender Connection*, ed. Anna Wilson (Cincinnati, Ohio: Anderson, 1993), p. 82.

38. *Statistics Packet*, 3rd ed., p. 182; "National Domestic Violence Awareness Month," p. H8486.

39. Tamar Lewin, "Case Might Fit Pattern of Abuse, Experts Say," *The New York Times*, June 19, 1994, p. 21.

40. Annie Gottlieb, "Whose Shocking Crime?" *The New York Times*, November 5, 1993, p. A35.

41. Ingrassia and Beck, pp. 30–31; Martin, p. 77; *Statistics Packet*, p. 189.

42. Patricia King, "Not So Different After All," *Newsweek*, October 4, 1993, p. 75; Achy Obejas, "Women Who Batter Women," *Ms.*, September/October 1994, p. 53.

43. Ingrassia and Beck, p. 31.

Chapter 4

1. "Call to Action Against Family Violence," *Hospitals*, November 5, 1992, p. 30.

2. "Disabled Man Abandoned," *The New York Times*, March 24, 1992, p. A12; Timothy Egan, "Old, Ailing and Finally a Burden Abandoned," *The New York Times*, March 26, 1992, pp. A1, B12; Frank Sabatino, "Elder Abuse: Abandonment Raising Public's Awareness," *Hospitals*, November 5, 1992, p. 29.

3. Joseph P. Shapiro, "The Elderly Are Not Children," *U.S. News & World Report*, January 13, 1992, pp. 26–28; "Help for the Terrified Elderly," *The New York Times*, April 2, 1991, p. A18.

4. "Domestic Mistreatment of the Elderly: Towards Prevention," *AARP*, pp. 1, 34.

5. Egan, p. A1.

6. Richard J. Gelles and Claire Pedrick Cornell, *Intimate Violence in Families*, 2nd ed. (Newbury Park, Calif.: Sage Publications, 1990), pp. 97–98; Kathleen M. Heide, *Why Kids Kill Parents: Child Abuse and Adolescent Homicide* (Columbus, Ohio: Ohio State University Press, 1992), p. 3.

7. Gelles and Cornell, pp. 98–99.

8. Heide, pp. 3, 44.

9. Ibid., pp. 44, 160.

10. Gelles and Cornell, pp. 85, 88.

11. Megan P. Goodwin and Bruce Roscoe, "Sibling Violence and Agonistic Interactions Among Middle Adolescents," *Adolescence*, vol. XXV, no. 98, Summer 1990, p. 453; Gelles and Cornell, p. 88; Goodwin and Roscoe, p. 464.

12. Gelles and Cornell, p. 89.

13. Teri Randall, "Adolescents May Experience Home, School Abuse; Their Future Draws Researchers' Concern," *JAMA*, June 17, 1992, p. 3127.

14. Naomi A. Adler and Joseph Schutz, "Sibling Incest Offenders," *Child Abuse and Neglect*, vol. 19, no. 7, 1995, pp. 811–812.

15. Ibid., p. 818.

16. Javad H. Kashani, Anasseril E. Daniel, Alison C. Dandoy, and William R. Holcomb, "Family Violence: Impact on Children," *Journal of the American Academy of Child and Adolescent Psychiatry*, March 1992, p. 185.

Chapter 5

1. Gloria Jacobs, "Where Do We Go From Here: An Interview with Ann Jones," *Ms.*, September/October 1994, p. 61.

2. Personal interview with Seriya Stone, January 19, 1996.

3. Suzanne K. Steinmetz, "The Violent Family," *Violence in the Home: Interdisciplinary Perspectives*, ed. Mary Lystad (New York: Brunner/Mazel Publishers, 1986), p. 54.

4. Joseph P. Shapiro, "The Elderly Are Not Children," *U.S. News & World Report*, January 13, 1992, p. 26.

5. Tamar Lewin, "A.M.A. Guidelines Ask Doctors to Help Identify Abuse of Elderly," *The New York Times*, November 24, 1992, p. A10.

6. Antonia C. Novello, Mark Rosenberg, Linda Saltzman, and John Shosky, "From the Surgeon General, US Public Health Service," *JAMA*, June 17, 1992, p. 3132.

7. Nancy Kathleen Sugg and Thomas Inui, "Primary Care Physicians' Response to Domestic Violence: Opening Pandora's Box," *JAMA*, June 17, 1992, p. 3158.

8. Council on Ethical and Judicial Affairs, American Medical Association, "Physicians and Domestic Violence: Ethical Considerations," *JAMA*, June 17, 1992, p. 3190.

9. Margaret Martin, "Battered Women," *The Violent Family: Victimization of Women, Children and Elders*, ed. Nancy Hutchings (New York: Human Sciences Press, 1988), p. 82; Joseph R. Biden, "Domestic Violence: A Crime, Not a Quarrel," *Trial*, June 1993, p. 56.

10. Personal interview with Diane Crosson, December 21, 1995.

11. Jill Smolowe, "When Violence Hits Home," *Time*, July 1, 1994; America Online: LonStr 75, May 29, 1995.

12. Janell D. Schmidt and Lawrence W. Sherman, "Does Arrest Deter Domestic Violence?" *American Behavioral Scientist*, vol. 36, no. 5, May 1993, p. 606.

13. Linda Hirshman, "Making Safety a Civil Right," *Ms.*, September/October 1994, p. 46.

14. Lourdes Rosado, "Who's Caring for Grandma?" *Newsweek*, July 29, 1991, p. 47.

15. Michele Ingrassia and Melinda Beck, "Patterns of Abuse," *Newsweek*, July 4, 1994, p. 32.

16. Hirshman, pp. 54–55.

17. Personal interview with Judith Cornelius, January 26, 1996.

18. Annie Gottlieb, "Whose Shocking Crime?" *The New York Times*, November 5, 1993, p. A35; Janet A. Geller, *Breaking Destructive Patterns: Multiple Strategies for Treating Partner Abuse* (New York: The Free Press, 1992).

19. Hirshman, pp. 54–55.

20. Personal interview with Char Bateman, December 22, 1995.

21. Personal interview with Diane Crosson, December 21, 1995.

22. Personal interview with Char Bateman, December 22, 1995.

23. Kathleen M. Heide, *Why Kids Kill Parents: Child Abuse and Adolescent Homicide* (Columbus, Ohio: Ohio State University Press, 1992), p. 155.

24. Ibid., p. 159.

25. Frank Sabatino, "50 Million People Watch Child Abuse Documentary," *Hospitals*, November 5, 1992, p. 28.

26. Jane Gross, "Simpson Case Galvanizes U.S. About Domestic Violence," *The New York Times*, July 4, 1994, p. 6.

27. Charlie Nobles, "Abuse of Women: 'Not O.K.,'" *The New York Times*, October 19, 1994, p. B17.

28. Heide, p. 159; George Lardner Jr., "1 in 3 Say They Have Seen Domestic Violence," *The Washington Post*, April 20, 1993, p. A7.

29. Personal interview with Wendy Varnell, January 11, 1996.

30. Personal interview with Seriya Stone, January 19, 1996.

Further Reading

Adler, Naomi A., and Joseph Schutz. "Sibling Incest Offenders." *Child Abuse and Neglect*, vol. 19, 1995, 811–819.

Allen, Robert L., and Paul Kivel. "Men Changing Men." *Ms.*, September/October 1994, 50–53.

Alvarez, Lizette. "Stepfather Is Indicted in Elisa's Case." *The New York Times*, January 26, 1996, B6.

Berkow, Ira. "Is Sports on Trial with O. J.?" *The New York Times*, July 7, 1994, B9.

Bernstein, Nina. "As Abuse Case Details Emerge, a Memo Harshly Assails Agency." *The New York Times*, December 5, 1995, A1.

Biden, Joseph R. "Domestic Violence: A Crime Not a Quarrel." *Trial*, June 1993, 56–62.

Bradley, Bill. "We Can't Hide Domestic Violence." *Philadelphia Inquirer*, September 26, 1994, A11.

Bradway, Becky. "Just the Facts . . . Child Sexual Abuse." *Coalition Commentary*, Summer 1993, 6–8.

Bray, Rosemary L. "Remember the Children." *Ms.*, September/October 1994, 38–43.

Bureau of Justice Statistics. *Report to the Nation on Crime and Justice*. Washington, DC: Department of Justice, 1983.

Burton, Dan. "When Violence Hits Home." *People*, April 4, 1994, 91–96.

"Call to Action Against Family Violence." *Hospitals*, November 5, 1992, 30.

Child Abuse and Neglect Fact Sheet. Washington, D.C.: National Clearinghouse on Child Abuse and Neglect Information.

"Children of Domestic Violence: Risks and Remedies." *Child Protective Services Quarterly*, Winter 1992, 1–4.

Council on Ethical and Judicial Affairs, American Medical Association. "Physicians and Domestic Violence: Ethical Considerations." *JAMA*, 267, June 17, 1992, 3190–3193.

Council on Scientific Affairs, American Medical Association. "Adolescents as Victims of Family Violence." *JAMA*, 270, October 20, 1993, 1850–1856.

Council on Scientific Affairs, American Medical Association. "Violence Against Women: Relevance for Medical Practicioners." *JAMA*, 267, June 17, 1992, 3184–3189.

Courts and Communities: Confronting Violence in the Family. Proceedings of State Justice Institute Conference. San Francisco: March 25–28, 1993.

Cowley, Geoffrey, with Ginny Carroll. "Stopping Abuse: What Works." *Newsweek*, July 4, 1994, 32–33.

D. G. "What's Love Got to Do with It?" *Ms.*, September/October 1994, 34–37.

"Disabled Man Abandoned." *The New York Times*, March 24, 1992, A12.

Domestic Mistreatment of the Elderly: Towards Prevention. Washington, DC: American Association of Retired Persons, 1995.

118

Egan, Timothy. "Old, Ailing and Finally a Burden Abandoned." *The New York Times*, March 26, 1992, A1, B12.

Ehrenreich, Barbara. "Oh, *Those* Family Values." *Time*, July 18, 1994, 62.

Ellis, David. "Bloody Obsessions: For Many Stalking Victims, Threats Are a Prelude to Murderous Violence." *People*, May 17, 1993, 71.

Ellis, Deborah. "Crime Bill Should Make Women Feel Safer." Letter. *The New York Times*, September 20, 1994, A22.

Emery, Robert E. "Family Violence." *American Psychologist*, February 1989, 321–328.

Facts About Child Abuse and Neglect. Washington, DC: National Council on Child Abuse & Family Violence (undated).

"Facts About Family Violence and Hospitals." *Hospitals*, November 5, 1992, 25.

Finkelhor, David. "Current Information on the Scope and Nature of Child Sexual Abuse." *The Future of Children*, 4, Summer/Fall 1994, 31–53.

————. "Prevention Approaches to Child Sexual Abuse." *Violence in the Home: Interdisciplinary Perspectives.* ed. Mary Lystad. New York: Brunner/Mazel Publishers, 1986, 296–308.

Geller, Janet A. *Breaking Destructive Patterns: Multiple Strategies for Treating Partner Abuse.* New York: The Free Press, 1992.

Gelles, Richard J., and Claire Pedrick Cornell. *Intimate Violence in Families.* 2nd ed. Newbury Park, CA: Sage Publications, 1990.

Gelles, Richard J., Regina Lackner, and Glenn D. Wolfner. "Risk-Markers of Men Who Batter, A 1994 Analysis." *Newsweek*, July 4, 1994, 29.

Glaser, Daniel. "Violence in the Society." *Violence in the Home: Interdisciplinary Perspectives*, ed. Mary Lystad. New York: Brunner/Mazel Publishers, 1986, 5–31.

Goleman, Daniel. "Standard Therapies May Help Only Impulsive Spouse Abuse." *The New York Times*, June 22, 1994, C11.

Goodwin, Megan P., and Bruce Roscoe. "Sibling Violence and Agonistic Interactions Among Middle Adolescents." *Adolescence*, XXV, Summer 1990, 451–467.

Gottlieb, Annie. "Whose Shocking Crime?" *The New York Times*, November 5, 1993, A35.

Gross, Jane. "Simpson Case Galvanizes U.S. About Domestic Violence." *The New York Times*, July 4, 1994, 6.

Hamilton, Julia. "Child Abuse and Family Violence." *The Violent Family: Victimization of Women, Children and Elders*, ed. Nancy Hutchings. New York: Human Sciences Press, 1988, 89–103.

Heide, Kathleen M. *Why Kids Kill Parents: Child Abuse and Adolescent Homicide*. Columbus, Ohio: Ohio State University Press, 1992.

"Help for the Terrified Elderly." *The New York Times*, April 2, 1992, A18.

Hirshman, Linda. "Making Safety a Civil Right." *Ms.*, September/October 1994, 44–49.

Hutchings, Nancy. Introduction. *The Violent Family: Victimization of Women, Children and Elders.* ed. Nancy Hutchings. New York: Human Sciences Press, 1988, 15–25.

Ingrassia, Michelle, and Melinda Beck. "Patterns of Abuse." *Newsweek,* July 4, 1994, 26–33.

Jacobs, Gloria. "Where Do We Go From Here: An Interview with Ann Jones." *Ms.,* September/October 1994, 56–63.

Kashani, Javad H., Anasseril E. Daniel, Alison C. Dandoy, and William R. Holcomb. "Family Violence: Impact on Children." *Journal of the American Academy of Child and Adolescent Psychiatry,* 31, March 1992, 181–189.

King, Patricia. "Not So Different After All." *Newsweek,* October 4, 1993, 75.

Kuehl, S. "Legal Remedies for Teen Dating Violence." *Dating Violence: Young Women in Danger.* Ed. Barrie Levy. Seattle: Seal Press, 1991.

Lardner, George, Jr. "1 in 3 Say They Have Seen Domestic Violence." *The Washington Post,* April 20, 1993, A7.

———. "Judges' Conference Hears of Family 'Terrorism.'" *The Washington Post,* April 4, 1993, A20.

———. "The Stalking of Kristin: The Law Made It Easy for My Daughter's Killer." *The Washington Post,* November 22, 1992, C1.

Lewin, Tamar. "A.M.A. Guidelines Ask Doctors to Help Identify Abuse of Elderly." *The New York Times,* November 24, 1992, A10.

———. "Case Might Fit Pattern of Abuse, Experts Say." *The New York Times,* June 19, 1994, 21.

————. "Two Polls Find Wide Abuse of Children." *Austin American-Statesman*, December 7, 1995, A1, A10.

Lystad, Mary. "Interdisciplinary Perspectives on Family Violence: An Overview." *Violence in the Home: Interdisciplinary Perspectives*, ed. Mary Lystad. New York: Brunner/Mazel Publishers, 1986, xi–xxxv.

Maraniss, David. *First in His Class: A Biography of Bill Clinton*. New York: Simon & Schuster, 1995.

Marks, Jane. "We Have a Problem." *Parents*, March 1990, 63–67.

Martin, Margaret. "Battered Women." *The Violent Family: Victimization of Women, Children and Elders*, 63–88.

Mason, James O., M.D., DrPH. "The Dimensions of Family Violence." *Public Health Reports*, 108, January/February 1993, 1–3.

Mather, Cynthia L., with Kristina E. Debye. *How Long Does It Hurt?* San Francisco: Jossey-Bass Publishers, 1994.

McCurdy, Karen, and Deborah Daro. *Current Trends in Child Abuse Reporting and Fatalities: The Results of the 1993 Annual Fifty State Survey*. Chicago: National Committee to Prevent Child Abuse, 1994.

Merz, Beverly. "Family Violence and the Physician." *American Medical News*, January 6, 1992, 3.

Metzger, Diane. "A Child Dies, and the System Tries to Hide Everyone's Problem." Letter. *The New York Times*, December 3, 1995, 14.

Monteleone, James A., Sheila Glaze, and Karen M. Bly. "Sexual Abuse: An Overview." *Child Maltreatment: A Clinical Guide and Reference*. St. Louis: G. W. Medical Publishing, 1994, 113–131.

"National Domestic Violence Awareness Month." *Congressional Record*, October 26, 1993, H8485–H8486.

Nelson, Mariah Burton. "Bad Sports." *The New York Times*, June 22, 1994, A21.

Nobles, Charlie. "Abuse of Women: 'Not O.K.'" *The New York Times*, October 19, 1994, B17.

Novello, Antonia C., Mark Rosenberg, Linda Saltzman, and John Shosky. "From the Surgeon General, US Public Health Service." *JAMA*, 267, June 17, 1992, 3132.

Obejas, Achy. "Women Who Batter Women." *Ms.*, September/October 1994, 53.

Peyser, Marc, with Carla Power. "The Death of Little Elisa." *Newsweek*, December 11, 1995, 42.

"Postnatal Causes of Developmental Disabilities in Children Aged 3-10 Years–Atlanta, Georgia, 1991." *U.S. Centers for Disease Control Morbidity and Mortality Weekly Report*, February 16, 1996, 130–134.

"Questions on a Child's Death." *The New York Times*, December 3, 1995, 2.

Quindlen, Anna. "Remember Nicole Simpson." *The New York Times*, June 22, 1994, A21.

Randall, Teri. "Adolescents May Experience Home, School Abuse: Their Future Draws Researchers' Concern." *JAMA*, 267, June 17, 1992, 3127–3131.

Rasche, Christine E. "'Given' Reasons for Violence in Intimate Relationships." *Homicide: The Victim/Offender Connection.* ed. Anna Wilson. Cincinnati, Ohio: Anderson, 1993, 82.

Rimer, Sara. "Handling of 1989 Wife-Beating Case Was a 'Terrible Joke,' Prosecutor Says." *The New York Times,* July 18, 1994, 10.

Rosado, Lourdes. "Who's Caring for Grandma?" *Newsweek,* July 29, 1991, 47.

Sabatino, Frank. "50 Million People Watch Child Abuse Documentary." *Hospitals,* November 5, 1992, 28.

———. "Elder Abuse: Abandonment Raising Public's Awareness." *Hospitals,* November 5, 1992, 29.

Schmidt, Janell D., and Lawrence W. Sherman. "Does Arrest Deter Domestic Violence?" *American Behavioral Scientist,* 36, May 1993, 601–609.

Shalala, Donna E. Speech. *NRCCSA News,* 2, January/February 1994, 1.

Shapiro, Joseph P. "The Elderly Are Not Children." *U.S. News & World Report,* January 13, 1992, 26–28.

Smolowe, Jill. "When Violence Hits Home." *Time,* July 1, 1994; America Online: LonStr 75, May 29, 1995.

State of Iowa. Supreme Court. *Final Report of the Supreme Court Task Force on Courts' and Communities' Response to Domestic Abuse.* August 1994.

Statistics Packet. 3rd ed. Philadelphia: National Clearinghouse for the Defense of Battered Women, 1994.

Steinmetz, Suzanne K. "The Violent Family." *Violence in the Home: Interdisciplinary Perspectives.* ed. Mary Lystad. New York: Brunner/Mazel Publishers, 1986, 51–70.

Sugg, Nancy Kathleen, and Thomas Inui. "Primary Care Physicians' Response to Domestic Violence: Opening Pandora's Box." *JAMA*, 267, June 17, 1992, 3157–3160.

Van Biema, David. "Abandoned to Her Fate; Neighbors, Teachers and the Authorities All Knew Elisa Izquierdo Was Being Abused. But Somehow Nobody Managed to Stop It." *Time*, December 11, 1995, 32.

"Violence Begins at Home." *The New York Times*, July 5, 1994, A16.

Walker, Lenore E. A. "Psychological Causes of Family Violence." *Violence in the Home: Interdisciplinary Perspectives*, ed. Mary Lystad. New York: Brunner/Mazel Publishers, 1986, 71–97.

Index

ERVIN TRASK MEM. LIBRARY
PLAINVILLE HIGH SCHOOL